ASP.NET Core 1.1 Web API
for Beginners

ASP.NET Core 1.1 MVC for Beginners - How to Build a Video Course Website

Overview 1

    Setup 2

    Other Titles by the Author 3

        Books by the Author 3

        Store Secret Data in .NET Core Web App with Azure Key Vault (video course) 4

        MVC 5 – How to Build a Membership Website (video course) 4

    Source Code and Bonus Materials 5

    Disclaimer – Who Is This Book for? 5

    Rights 6

    About the Author 6

Part 1: Introduction to ASP.NET Core 1.1 Web API 9

1. Introduction 11

    Introduction 11

    What Is ASP.NET Core? 11

    What Is the .NET Core Framework? 11

    What Is .NET Standard? 12

    Full .NET Framework vs. .NET Core 12

    Creating the Solution and Project 12

        Important Files 15

            Program.cs 15

            Other Files 16

        Compiling the Solution 17

        The Startup.cs File 18

    Reading from a Configuration File 19

    Reading from the Secrets.Json File 22

    Summary 24

2. Middleware 25

    Introduction.. 25

    How Does Middleware Work? 25

    IApplicationBuilder 26

        Handling Exceptions 28

    Installing Postman 31

    Setting Up ASP.NET MVC/Web API 32

        Adding the MVC NuGet Package 32

    Summary.. 35

3. Controllers 37

    Introduction.. 37

    Routing 38

    HTTP Verbs and HTTP Attributes.. 41

    Summary.. 42

4. Models.. 43

    Introduction.. 43

    POCO Models... 43

    Data Annotations... 45

    Summary.. 46

Part 2: ASP.NET Core 1.1 Web API Using In-Memory Data 47

5. Adding In-Memory Data Storage... 49

    Introduction.. 49

    Creating the Main DTOs 50

    Creating the In-Memory Data Collections................................. 51

    Summary.. 53

6. Adding an In-Memory Data Service... 55

    Introduction.. 55

Adding the BookstoreMockRepository Data Service 56

Summary.. 58

7. Adding the Publishers Controller.. 59

Introduction... 59

Status Codes 59

Adding the Publishers Controller 61

Get a List of Publishers (GET) 62

Get a Single Publisher (GET) 66

Adding the GetPublisher Method to the Service 67

Calling the GetPublisher Method from the Controller.. 68

Add Status Code Pages 73

Add a Publisher (POST).. 74

Adding the PublisherCreateDTO Class... 75

Adding the AddPublisher Method to the Service... 76

Adding the Save Method to the Service.. 77

Adding the Post Action to the PublishersController Class 78

Update a Publisher (PUT) 82

Adding the PublisherUpdateDTO Class 82

Adding the UpdatePublisher Method to the Service 83

Adding the PublisherExists Method to the Service 84

Adding the Put Action to the PublishersController Class 85

Partially Update a Publisher (PATCH) 88

Delete a Publisher (DELETE) 92

Adding the DeleteBook Method to the Service 92

Adding the DeletePublisher Method to the Service... 93

Adding the Delete Action Method in the PublishersController Class 94

Summary... 97

8. Adding the Books Controller 99

Introduction.. 99

Adding the BooksController Class 100

Get a List of Books (GET) 101

Adding the GetBooks Method to the IBookstoreRepository Interface 101

Adding the Get Action Method to the BooksController Class................................ 102

Get a Book (GET)... 104

Adding the GetBook Method to the IBookstoreRepository Interface 104

Adding the Get Action Method to the BooksController Class................................ 105

Add a Book (POST).. 106

Adding the BookCreateDTO Class 107

Adding the AddBook Method to the Service... 108

Adding the Post Action to the BooksController Class 109

Update a Book (PUT) 112

Adding the BookUpdateDTO Class 112

Adding the UpdateBook Method to the Service 113

Adding the Put Action to the BooksController Class................................... 114

Partial Update of a Book (PATCH) 117

Delete a Book (DELETE) 120

Summary... 122

Part 3: Creating an Entity Framework Service... 123

9. Entity Classes 125

Introduction.. 125

Adding the Publisher and Book Entity Classes 125

Summary... 128

10. Entity Framework and AutoMapper.. 129

Introduction.. 129

Installing Entity Framework and User Secrets... 129

    Adding the SqlDbContext Class 131

    Configuration in the Startup Class... 132

    Adding the Initial Migration and Creating the Database........................... 134

Installing AutoMapper... 136

Configuring AutoMapper... 138

Adding the BookstoreSqlRepository Service Component 139

    Implementing the BookstoreSqlRepository Service Component Class................... 139

Using the BookstoreSqlRepository Service Component 146

    Fetching All Publishers... 147

    Fetching One Publisher.. 148

    Fetching a Publisher with Its Related Books.. 148

    Fetching a Non-Existing Publisher 149

    Adding a Publisher... 149

    Updating a Publisher 151

    Partially Updating a Publisher 153

    Deleting a Publisher... 155

    Fetching All Books Related to a Publisher 157

    Fetching a Specific Book Related to a Publisher.. 158

    Fetching a Non-Existing Book 158

    Adding a Book... 158

    Updating a Book 160

    Partially Updating a Book 161

    Deleting a Book... 163

Summary.. 164

Part 4: Creating a Generic Entity Framework Service 165

11. Adding a Generic EF Data Service... 167

Introduction...167

Creating the Generic Service and the Controller classes 168

Summary...171

12. Implementing the Generic Service 173

Introduction...173

The Get<TEntity> Method (Collection) 174

Adding the Get<TEntity> Method to the Service 174

Fetching all Publishers (GET) 175

Fetching all Books (GET) 176

The Get<TEntity> Method (One)...177

Adding the Get<TEntity> Method to the Service 178

Fetching One Publisher (GET)..180

Fetching One Book (GET)...182

The Save Method..183

The Add<TEntity> Method 184

Add a Publisher (POST)..185

Add a Book (POST)...187

Updating an Entity..189

Updating a Publisher (PUT) 189

Updating a Book (PUT) 191

Partially Updating a Publisher (PATCH) 193

Partially Updating a Book (PATCH)..196

Adding the Exists<TEntity> Method to the Service 198

The Delete<TEntity> Method 199

Adding the Delete Method to the Service..199

Deleting a Publisher (DELETE) 200

Deleting a Book (DELETE) 201

Summary... 203

Other Titles by the Author.. 205

Books by the Author 205

Store Secret Data in .NET Core Web App with Azure Key Vault (video course)...... 206

MVC 5 – How to Build a Membership Website (video course) 206

Overview

I would like to welcome you to *ASP.NET Core 1.1 Web API for Beginners*. This book will guide you through creating your very first Web API application. It is not a beginner book in the sense that it teaches you C# from the ground up; it's a beginner course on how to build a Web API. To get the most from this book, you should have a good understanding of the C# language, such as object-oriented programming (OOP), generics, and reflection; in other words, you should be an intermediate C# developer.

The tools used in this book: Visual Studio 2017 (any version), Postman (to send requests to the Web APIs action methods and receive the returned responses), ASP.NET Core 1.1, and Entity Framework Core 1.1.

The book will have four parts: The first part is an introduction to ASP.NET Core 1.1 Web API. In the second part, you will learn how to create a Web API that uses in-memory data, collections, to learn how to get, add, update, and delete data. In the third part, you will use the same Web API controller and actions and switch to using Entity Framework Core and SQL Server to manipulate data. In the last part of the book you will build a service that uses a generic interface and class to manipulate data with Entity Framework Core in the database you created earlier. You will use generics and reflection when implementing the service.

Because this is a book on how to create your first Web API, you won't be building a user interface to display and maniupulate the data. You will instead use a tool called Postman to call the actions in the Web API controllers.

ASP.NET Core is a new framework from Microsoft. It has been designed from the ground up to be fast and flexible, and to work across multiple platforms. ASP.NET Core is the framework to use for your future ASP.NET applications.

The application you build following the examples in this book will evolve into a basic Web API, starting with an empty template. You will add the necessary pieces one at a time to get a good understanding of how things fit together. The focus is on building a Web API by installing and configuring middleware, services, and other frameworks.

You will install middleware to create a processing pipeline, and then look at the MVC framework, which also is used when creating Web APIs. If you already are familiar with MVC or Web API from previous versions of ASP.NET, you will notice some similarities.

You will work with Entity Framework Core to store and retrieve data, and install Auto-Mapper to transform one object into another to cut down the amount of code you write. Note that dependency injection now is a first-class design pattern. You will therefore use it to access necessary service functionality in the Web API controllers you add.

By the end of this book you will be able to create a simple ASP.NET Core 1.1 Web API application on your own, which can create, edit, delete, and get data from a database.

The application you will build will revolve around publishers and books. The first controller will use in-memory data added to collections. Then you will use the same interface to create a new implementation that uses Entity Framework Core to fetch data from a database. You will then add controllers that will use a generic service implementation to access data from the database. Using generics will allow you to reuse the same code for all the tables in the database. Reflection will be necessary in one of the method implementations to find out the related entities of a parent entity.

Setup

In this book, you will be using C# and any Visual Studio 2017 version that you have access to. You can even use the free Visual Studio Community 2017 version, which you can download from www.visualstudio.com/downloads.

You can develop ASP.NET Core applications on Mac OS X and Linux, but then you are restricted to the ASP.NET Core libraries that don't depend on .NET Framework, which requires Windows.

The applications in this book require ASP.NET Core 1.1.x.

You will install additional libraries using NuGet packages when necessary throughout the book.

The complete code is available on GitHub with a commit for each task.

Link to the code: https://github.com/csharpschool/AspNetCoreWebAPI

Errata: https://github.com/csharpschool/AspNetCoreWebAPI/issues

Book version: 1.0

Other Titles by the Author
The author has written other books and produced video courses that you might find helpful.

Books by the Author
Below is a list if the most recent books by the author. The books are available on Amazon.

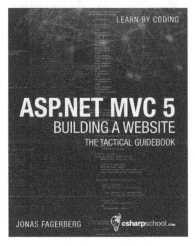 

ASP.NET Core 1.1 – Building a Website: http://www.amazon.com/dp/1546832068

ASP.NET MVC 5 – Building a Website: www.amazon.com/dp/B01IF63FIY

C# for Beginners: https://www.amazon.com/dp/B017OAFR8I

Store Secret Data in .NET Core Web App with Azure Key Vault (video course)

In this Udemy course you will learn how to store sensitive data in a secure manner. First you will learn how to store data securely in a file called *secrets.json* with the User Manager. The file is stored locally on your machine, outside the project's folder structure. It is therefore not checked into your code repository. Then you will learn how to use Azure Web App Settings to store key-value pairs for a specific web application. The third and final way to secure your sensitive data is using Azure Key Vault, secured with Azure Active Directory in the cloud.

The course is taught using an ASP.NET Core 1.1 Web API solution in Visual Studio 2015 and Visual Studio 2017.

You really need to know this if you are a serious developer.

You can watch this video course on Udemy at this URL:
www.udemy.com/store-secret-data-in-net-core-web-app-with-azure-key-vault

MVC 5 – How to Build a Membership Website (video course)

This is a comprehensive video course on how to build a membership site using ASP.NET MVC 5. The course has more than **24 hours** of video.

In this video course, you will learn how to build a membership website from scratch. You will create the database using Entity Framework code-first, scaffold an Administrator UI, and build a front-end UI using HTML5, CSS3, Bootstrap, JavaScript, C#, and MVC 5. Prerequisites for this course are: a good knowledge of the C# language and basic knowledge of MVC 5, HTML5, CSS3, Bootstrap, and JavaScript.

You can watch this video course on Udemy at this URL:
www.udemy.com/building-a-mvc-5-membership-website

Source Code and Bonus Materials

The source code accompanying this book is shared under the MIT License and can be downloaded on GitHub, with a commit for each task.

Link to the code: https://github.com/csharpschool/AspNetCoreWebAPI

Errata: https://github.com/csharpschool/AspNetCoreWebAPI/issues

Disclaimer – Who Is This Book for?

It's important to mention that this book is not meant to be a *get-to-know-it-all* book; it's more on the practical and tactical side, where you will learn as you progress through the exercises and build a real application in the process. Because I personally dislike having to read hundreds upon hundreds of pages of irrelevant fluff (filler material) not necessary for the tasks at hand, and also view it as a disservice to the readers, I will assume that we are of the same mind on this, and will therefore only include important information pertinent for the tasks at hand, thus making the book both shorter and more condensed and also saving you time and effort in the process. Don't get me wrong, I will describe the important things in great detail, leaving out only the things that are not directly relevant to your first experience with an ASP.NET Core 1.1 Web API Application. The goal is for you to have created a working Web API application upon finishing this book. You can always look into details at a later time when you have a few projects under your belt. ***If you prefer encyclopedic books describing everything in minute detail with short examples, and value a book by how many pages it has, rather than its content, then this book is NOT for you***.

The examples in this book are presented using the free Visual Studio 2017 Community version and ASP.NET Core 1.1. You can download Visual Studio 2017 here:
www.visualstudio.com/downloads

Rights

About the Author

Jonas started a company back in 1994 focusing on teaching Microsoft Office and the Microsoft operating systems. While still studying at the University of Skovde in 1995, he wrote his first book about Widows 95, as well as a number of course materials.

In the year 2000, after working as a Microsoft Office developer consultant for a couple of years, he wrote his second book about Visual Basic 6.0.

Between 2000 and 2004, he worked as a Microsoft instructor with two of the largest educational companies in Sweden, teaching Visual Basic 6.0. When Visual Basic.NET and C# were released, he started teaching those languages, as well as the .NET Framework. He was also involved in teaching classes at all levels, from beginner to advanced developers.

From the year 2005, Jonas shifted his career towards consulting once again, working hands-on with the languages and framework he taught.

Jonas wrote his third book, *C# Programming*, aimed at beginner to intermediate developers in 2013, and in 2015 his fourth book, *C# for Beginners – The Tactical Guide*, was published. Shortly thereafter his fifth book, *ASP.NET MVC 5 – Building a Website: The Tactical Guidebook*, was published. In 2017 his sixth and seventh books, *ASP.NET Core 1.1 – Building a Website for Beginners* and *ASP.NET Core 1.1 – Building a Web API for Beginners*, were published.

Jonas has also produced a 24h+ video course titled Building an ASP.NET MVC 5 Membership Website (www.udemy.com/building-a-mvc-5-membership-website), showing in great detail how to build a membership website.

ASP.NET Core 1.1 Web API for Beginners

And a course on how to secure sensitive data in web applications, titled <u>Store Secret Data in a .NET Core Web App with Azure Key Vault</u>, is also available on Udemy.

All the books and video courses, including **C# for Beginners – The Tactical Guide**, **MVC 5 – How to Build a Membership Website (book and video)**, **Store Secret Data in a .NET Core Web App with Azure Key Vault, ASP.NET Core 1.1 for Beginners**, and this book, have been specifically written with the student in mind.

Part 1:
Introduction to ASP.NET
Core 1.1 Web API

1. Introduction

Introduction

Let's start by describing what ASP.NET Core is before you create your first Web API application.

What Is ASP.NET Core?

ASP.NET Core is an open-source, cross-platform framework for building cloud-based, internet-connected solutions. It can be web apps and Web APIs for those apps as well as for mobile apps. You can find the ASP.NET Core code at https://github.com/aspnet.

Because it is cross-platform enabled, you can develop on and run your applications on Windows, Linux, and Mac operating systems. The latter two require you to use ASP.NET Core and Entity Framework Core; you can't use older versions of Entity Framework or ASP.NET since they require Windows to work.

You can use any version of Visual Studio 2017, Visual Studio Code, or any other editor of your choice. The examples in this book are created using Visual Studio 2017 and Windows 10.

ASP.NET Core is not an update from the previous version of ASP.NET; it was rewritten from the ground up to make it more granular and flexible, using NuGet packages to install only the functionality you need. Some benefits to this approach are: smaller application surface area, tighter security, and improved performance.

What Is the .NET Core Framework?

The .NET Core framework is a modular and portable cross-platform framework that is designed for code sharing and reuse. It's a sub-set of the full .NET Framework that can be used regardless of the platform you target, which means that you only have to write and maintain one version of your code.

You can use .NET Core with web applications on Windows, Linux and Mac, Windows desktop applications, Windows devices, and phone apps, and in the future, you will be able to use it with Xamarin.

.NET Core is released through NuGet packages, which makes it modular, just like ASP.NET Core. You can install the functionality you need, instead of one large monolithic assembly.

What Is .NET Standard?

The .NET Standard is not a downloadable framework; it's a standard that defines a common base-layer that a platform should support. .NET Core is Microsoft's implementation of that standard.

Full .NET Framework vs. .NET Core

Using the full .NET Framework makes it possible to use the framework dependencies you are used to from earlier versions. This is not possible with .NET Core since it is a subset of the full framework.

That said, you would gain a lot by using .NET Core: modularity, a small footprint, performance improvements, and being able to run the application cross-platform.

Unless you need the functionality of the full .NET Framework, the suggested choice is to use .NET Core.

In this book, you will be using ASP.NET Core to build a Web API.

Creating the Solution and Project

In this book, you will be using C# and any Visual Studio 2017 version that you have access to. You can even use the free Visual Studio Community 2017 version, which you can down-load from www.visualstudio.com/downloads.

Now that you have Visual Studio 2017 installed on your computer, it's time to create your first project.

1. Open Visual Studio 2017.
2. Select **File-New-Project** (Ctrl+Shift+N) in the main menu.
3. Make sure that the **Templates-Visual C#-Web** node is selected in the **New Project** dialog.
   There are three templates available:
   a. ASP.NET Web Application (.NET Framework)
      Can be used to create traditional ASP.NET web applications (without .NET Core).

   b. ASP.NET Core Web Application (.NET Core)
       Can be used to create cross-platform ASP.NET Core web applications
       without the .NET Framework (not restricted to Windows).
   c. ASP.NET Core Web Application (.NET Framework)
       Can be used to create ASP.NET Core web applications dependent on
       .NET Framework (not cross-platform).
4. Select the **ASP.NET Core Web Application (.NET Core)** template.
5. Give the application a name and select which folder to place it in. You can name
   it *AspNetCorePublisherWebAPI*.
6. Make sure that the **Create directory for solution** checkbox is checked.
7. Learning how to use GitHub is not part of this course, so if you are unfamiliar
   with GitHub, you should make sure that the **Create new Git repository** checkbox
   is unchecked.
8. Click the **OK** button.

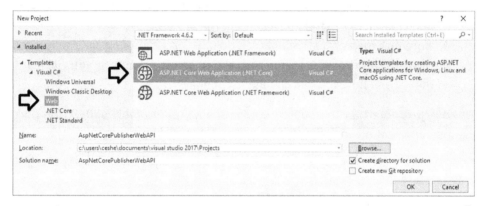

9. In the next dialog, make sure that the **ASP.NET Core 1.1** framework is selected at
   the top left of the dialog.
10. Select the **Empty** template to start from scratch without any pre-installed
    dependencies.
11. Click the **OK** button.

12. When the solution has been created in the folder you selected, it will contain all the files in the *AspNetCorePublisherWebAPI* project.
13. Press Ctrl+F5 on the keyboard, or select **Debug-Start Without Debugging** in the main menu, to run the application in the browser.
14. Note that the application only can do one thing right now, and that is to display the text *Hello World!* Later in this, and upcoming chapters, you will learn why that is, and how you can change that behavior.

For now, just note that the application is running on *localhost:55098* (the port number might be different on your machine).

If you right click on the IIS icon in the system tray, you can see that ISS is hosting the *AspNetCorePublisherWebAPI* application.

Important Files

There are a couple of files that you need to be aware of in ASP.NET Core 1.1, and some of these have changed from previous versions.

Program.cs

If you open the *Program.cs* file, you will see that it looks like a Console application you might have created in the past, and that is because an ASP.NET Core application is a Console application that calls into ASP.NET-specific libraries.

```
public static void Main(string[] args)
{
    var host = new WebHostBuilder()
        .UseKestrel()
        .UseContentRoot(Directory.GetCurrentDirectory())
        .UseIISIntegration()
        .UseStartup<Startup>()
        .UseApplicationInsights()
        .Build();

    host.Run();
}
```

The **Main** method in the **Program** class configures and runs the application. In it a **WebHostBuilder** instance is created to host the application using Kestrel, which is a cross-platform web server. Because you are running on Visual Studio, IIS will be used as the default web host. The **UseIISIntegration** method is called to use ISS Express as a reverse proxy server for Kestrel. Use IIS for applications that will run on a Windows server, and a proxy such as Apache for Linux. You can self-host a web application with Kestrel alone, but that means that you will miss out on benefits from using IIS as a proxy.

The **UseContentRoot** method specifies the root of your web application. Note that it isn't the same as the web root, which is the content root followed by */wwwroot*.

The **UseStartup** method specifies the startup type to be used by the web host, which by default is the **Startup** class that was added when the application was created.

The Build method then builds the **WebHostBuilder** instance that will host the application, and the **Run** method starts the application and blocks the calling thread until the host shuts down.

Other Files

The **Properties** folder in the Solution Explorer contains a file called *launchSettings.json*, which contains all the settings needed to launch the application. It contains IIS settings, as well as project settings, such as environment variables and the application URL.

One major change from ASP.NET Core 1.0 is that the *project.json* file no longer exists; instead the installed NuGet packages are listed in the *.csproj* file. It can be opened and edited directly from Visual Studio (which is another change) or its content can be changed using the NuGet Package Manager.

After making changes to this file, you should restart Visual Studio to make sure that the changes have been loaded with the project.

To open the *.csproj* file, you simply right click on it and select **Edit AspNetCorePublisher-WebAPI.csproj** (substitute *AspNetCorePublisherWebAPI* with the name of the project you are in).

You can add NuGet packages by adding **PackageReference** nodes to the file *.csproj,* or by opening the NuGet Package Manager. Right click on the **project node** or the **References** node, and select **Manage NuGet Packages** to open the NuGet Manager.

Open the *.csproj* file and the NuGet manager side by side and compare them. As you can see, the same packages are listed in the dialog and in the file.

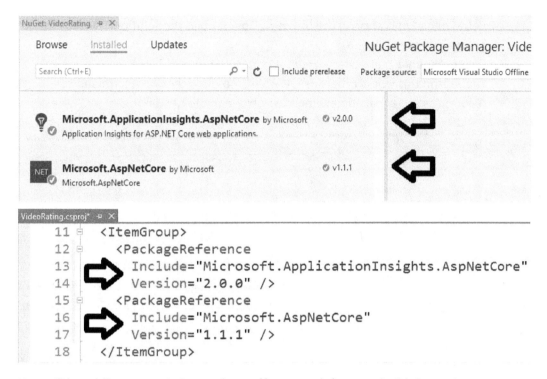

```
11 □   <ItemGroup>
12 □     <PackageReference
13         Include="Microsoft.ApplicationInsights.AspNetCore"
14         Version="2.0.0" />
15 □     <PackageReference
16         Include="Microsoft.AspNetCore"
17         Version="1.1.1" />
18     </ItemGroup>
```

You will be adding more NuGet packages (frameworks) as you build the project.

Compiling the Solution

It is important to know that ASP.NET will monitor the file system and recompile the application when files are changed and saved. Because ASP.NET monitors the file system and recompiles the code, you can use any text editor you like, such as Visual Studio Code, when building your applications. You are no longer bound to Visual Studio; all you need to do is to get the application running in the web server (IIS). Let's illustrate it with an example.

1. Start the application without debugging (Ctrl+F5) to get it running in IIS, if it isn't already open in a browser.
2. Open the *Startup.cs* file with Notepad (or any text editor) outside of Visual Studio. This file is responsible for configuring your application when it starts.
3. Locate the line of code with the string *Hello World*. This line of code is responsible for responding to every HTTP request in your application.
   ```
   await context.Response.WriteAsync("Hello World!");
   ```
4. Change the text to *Hello, from My World!* and save the file.
   ```
   await context.Response.WriteAsync("Hello, from My World!");
   ```

5. Refresh the application in the browser. Do not build the solution in Visual Studio before refreshing the page.
6. The text should change from *Hello World!* to *Hello, from My World!*
   The reason this works is because ASP.NET monitors the file system and recompiles the application when changes are made to a file.

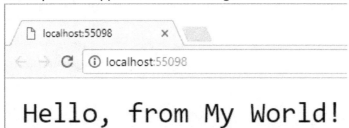

As mentioned earlier you can create cross-platform applications using ASP.NET Core 1.1, but this requires the *.NET Core* template. As of this writing, this template has limitations compared with the *.NET Framework* template. This, because .NET Framework contains features that are relying on the Windows operating system. In a few years' time, this gap will probably not be as significant, as the .NET Core platform evolves. So, if you don't need the added features in .NET Framework, then use the *.NET Core* template, as it is much leaner and cross-platform ready.

The Startup.cs File

Gone are the days when the *web.config* file ruled the configuration universe. Now the *Startup.cs* file contains a **Startup** class, which ASP.NET will look for by convention. The application and its configuration sources are configured in that class.

The **Configure** and **ConfigureServices** methods in the **Startup** class handle most of the application configuration. The HTTP processing pipeline is created in the **Configure** method, located at the end of the class. The pipeline defines how the application responds to requests; by default, the only thing it can do is to print *Hello World!* to the browser.

If you want to change this behavior, you will have to add additional code to the pipeline in this method. If you for instance want to serve up static files, like HTML or JSON, you will need to add that behavior to the pipeline.

If you want to add a pretty error page, or handle route request in an ASP.NET MVC/Web API application, you need to modify the pipeline.

The **Configure** method is where you set up the application's inversion of control container, which will be covered in more detail later in the book.

The second method in the **Startup** class is **ConfigureServices**, which is used to configure the application services.

You will learn more about how to configure your application in upcoming chapters.

For now, all you need to know about dependency injection is that, instead of creating instances of a class explicitly, they can be handed to a component when asked for. This makes your application loosely coupled and flexible.

Reading from a Configuration File

Let's say that the hardcoded string *Hello, from My World* is a string that shouldn't be hardcoded, and you want to read it from a configuration file. To solve this, you could implement a configuration source that fetches the value when asked. One place to store configuration data is the *appsettings.json* file.

Although printing data from a configuration source to the browser isn't directly applicable in a Web API, it will show you how to read from a configuration file. In the next section, you will read from a JSON file that is used to store sensitive data that you don't want to check into the code repository.

When the application is published to Azure, the key-value pairs in the Azure application settings for your project will be merged with the values in the *appsettings.json* file.

Let's implement this scenario in your application.

1. Right click on the project folder and select **Add-New Item**.
2. Search for *JSON* in the dialog's search field.
3. Select the **ASP.NET Configuration File** template.
4. Make sure the name of the file is *appsettings.json*. The file could be named anything, but *appsettings* is convention for this type of configuration file.
5. Click the **Add** button.
6. As you can see, a default connection string is already in the file. Remove the **ConnectionStrings** property and add the following key-value pair: *"Message":"Hello, from configuration"*. This is the file content after you have changed it.
    `{ "Message": "Hello, from configuration" }`

7. To read configuration information from the *appsettings.json* file, you have to add a constructor to the **Startup** class. You can do that by typing *ctor* in the class and hit the **Tab** key twice.

```
public class Startup
{
    public Startup()
    {
    }
    ...
}
```

8. You need to create an instance of the **ConfigurationBuilder** class called **builder** in the constructor, and chain on the **SetBasePath** method with the application's current directory as an argument. Without specifying the base path, the application will not know where to search for files.

```
var builder = new ConfigurationBuilder()
    .SetBasePath(Directory.GetCurrentDirectory());
```

9. To read the *appsettings.json* file you need to chain on the **AddJsonFile** method, with *appsettings.json* as an argument, to the **builder** object. If you need to include more files, you can chain on the method multiple times.

```
var builder = new ConfigurationBuilder()
    .SetBasePath(Directory.GetCurrentDirectory())
    .AddJsonFile("appsettings.json");
```

10. Add a property called **Configuration**, of type **IConfiguration**, to the **Startup** class. To get access to the interface you have to add a **using** statement to the **Microsoft.Extensions.Configuration** namespace.

```
public IConfiguration Configuration { get; set; }
```

11. Now, you need to build the configuration structure from the **ConfigurationBuilder** object, and store it in the **Configuration** property. You do this by calling the **Build** method on the **builder** variable in the constructor.

```
Configuration = builder.Build();
```

12. To replace the hardcoded text *Hello, from My World!* With the value stored in the **Message** property in the *appsettings.json* file, you have to index into the **Configuration** property. Store the value in a variable named **message** in the **Configure** method.

```
var message = Configuration["Message"];
```

13. Now, replace the hardcoded text with the variable.

```
await context.Response.WriteAsync(message);
```

14. Save all the files and go to the browser. Refresh the application to see the new message.

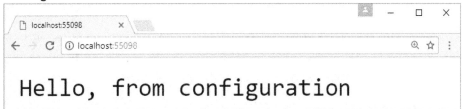

The **Startup** class's code, so far:

```
public class Startup
{
    public IConfiguration Configuration { get; set; }

    public Startup() {
        var builder = new ConfigurationBuilder()
            .SetBasePath(Directory.GetCurrentDirectory())
            .AddJsonFile("appsettings.json");

        Configuration = builder.Build();
    }

    public void Configure(IApplicationBuilder app,
    IHostingEnvironment env, ILoggerFactory loggerFactory)
    {
        loggerFactory.AddConsole();

        if (env.IsDevelopment())
        {
            app.UseDeveloperExceptionPage();
        }

        app.Run(async (context) =>
        {
            var message = Configuration["Message"];
            await context.Response.WriteAsync(message);
        });
    }
}
```

Reading from the Secrets.Json File

There are many ways to store configuration data locally in an ASP.NET Core 1.1 application. If you want to be certain that the data won't get checked into the code repository, there is only one safe place to store that data, in the *secrets.json* file. This JSON file is added to a cache folder outside the application folder structure. A project folder will be created in the *C:\Users\YourUserName\AppData\Roaming\Microsoft\UserSecrets* folder when User Secrets is activated in the project. The *UserSecrets* folder will contain a folder for each project where User Secrets has been activated.

Use the *secrets.json* to store sensitive data that you don't want checked into the code repository, such as passwords and connection strings.

Note that if you use the same key-name in the *secrets.json* file as in the *appsettings.json* file, the value from the *secrets.json* file will take precedence.

Also note that the values in the *secrets.json* file only are available locally on your machine and not from a published web application.

Although you are printing the value to the browser in this example, the same code will be used later in the book from a Web API controller.

Let's implement this scenario in your application.

1. Install the necessary NuGet packages in the *.csproj* file, either by typing in the package information in the *.csproj* file manually or by using the NuGet Package Manager. Listed below are the packages that you need to add to be able to read from the *secrets.json* file.

```
<ItemGroup>
    <PackageReference
        Include="Microsoft.Extensions.Configuration.UserSecrets"
        Version="1.1.2" />
</ItemGroup>

<ItemGroup>
    <DotNetCliToolReference
        Include="Microsoft.Extensions.SecretManager.Tools"
        Version="1.0.1" />
</ItemGroup>
```

2. Save all files and restart Visual Studio.

3. Right click on the project name in the Solution Explorer and select **Manage User Secrets**.

4. Add the following key-value pair to the *secrets.json* file that has been opened. Note that it is the same key-name that you used in the *appsettings.json* file.
```
{
    "Message": "Hello, from secrets.json"
}
```

5. Open the *Startup.cs* file.

6. Inject an instance of the **IHostingEnvironment** named **env** into the constructor by adding it as a parameter.
```
public Startup(IHostingEnvironment env) {
    ...
}
```

7. Use the **env** parameter to check if the current hosting environment is in **Development** mode above the **builder.Build** method call. It's the same code used in the **Configure** method. You can change the mode in the project's **Properties** dialog under the **Debug** tab.
```
if (env.IsDevelopment()) {
    ...
}
```

8. Add the User Secrets configuration source inside the if-block you just added by calling the **AddUserSecrets** method on the **builder** object.
```
builder.AddUserSecrets<Startup>();
```

9. Save all the files and start the application without debugging (Ctrl+F5). The text from *secrets.json* will be displayed in the browser.

The complete code for the constructor in **Setup.cs**:

```
public Startup(IHostingEnvironment env)
{
    var builder = new ConfigurationBuilder()
        .SetBasePath(Directory.GetCurrentDirectory())
        .AddJsonFile("appsettings.json");

    if (env.IsDevelopment())
    {
        builder.AddUserSecrets<Startup>();
    }

    Configuration = builder.Build();
}
```

Summary

In this chapter, you created your first ASP.NET Core 1.1 application and added only the necessary pieces to get it up and running. Throughout the book you will add new functionality to this project using services and middleware.

You also added and read from two configuration files, *appsettings.json* and *secrets.json*. You learned that the *secrets.json* file is the preferred method of storing sensitive data locally, and that it will take precedence over the *appsettings.json* file locally if the same key-names are used in both files.

In the next chapter, you will learn about middleware.

2. Middleware

Introduction

In this chapter, you will add middleware that handles HTTP requests, and how the application behaves if there is an error. One key aspect of the middleware is to perform user authentication and authorization.

By the end of this chapter you will have built a middleware pipeline for a MVC/Web API application.

How Does Middleware Work?

Let's have a look at how middleware works and what it is used for.

When an HTTP request comes to the server, it is the middleware components that handle that request.

Each piece of middleware in ASP.NET Core is an object with a very limited, specific, and focused role. This means that you will have to add many middleware components for an application to work properly.

The following example illustrates what can happen when an HTTP POST request to a URL, ending with /reviews, reaches the server.

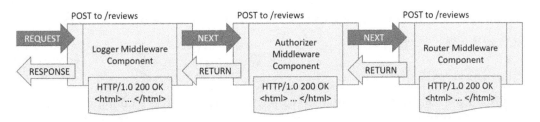

Logging is a separate middleware component that you might want to use to log information about every incoming HTTP request. It can see every piece of data, such as the headers, the query string, cookies, and access tokens. Not only can it read data from the request, it can also change information about it, and/or stop processing the request.

The most likely scenario with a logger is that it will log information and pass the processing onto the next middleware component in the pipeline.

This means that middleware is a series of components executed in order.

The next middleware component might be an authorizer that can look at access tokens or cookies to determine if the request will proceed. If the request doesn't have the correct credentials, the authorizer middleware component can respond with an HTTP error code or redirect the user to a login page.

If the request is authorized, it will be passed to the next middleware component, which might be a routing component. The router will look at the URL to determine where to go next, by looking in the application for something that can respond. A method in a controller class could be called, returning JSON, XML, or an HTML page for instance. If it can't find anything that can respond, the component could throw a *404 Not Found* error.

Let's say that it found an HTML page to respond, then the pipeline starts to call all the middleware components in reverse order, passing along the HTML. When the response ultimately reaches the first component, which is the logger in our example, it might log the time the request took and then allow the response to go back over the network to the client's browser.

This is what middleware is, a way to configure how the application should behave. A series of components that handle specific, narrow tasks, such as handle errors, serve up static files and send HTTP requests to the MVC framework. The MVC framework is also used when building Web API applications, and will make it possible for you to build the example publisher and book application.

This book will not go into the nitty-gritty of middleware, only the basics that you need to build a Web API application.

IApplicationBuilder

The **IApplicationBuilder** interface injected into the **Startup** class's **Configure** method is used when setting up the middleware pipeline.

```
public void Configure(IApplicationBuilder app, IHostingEnvironment env,
ILoggerFactory loggerFactory, IMessageService msg)
{
    loggerFactory.AddConsole();

    if (env.IsDevelopment())
        app.UseDeveloperExceptionPage();
```

```
    app.Run(async (context) =>
    {
        var message = Configuration["Message"];
        await context.Response.WriteAsync(message);
    });
}
```

To add middleware, you call extension methods on the **app** parameter, which contains the dependency-injected object for the **IApplicationBuilder** interface. Two middleware components are already defined in the **Configure** method.

The **UseDeveloperExceptionPage** middleware component will display a pretty error page to the developer, but not the user; you can see that it is encapsulated inside an if-block that checks if the environment variable is set to the development environment.

The **UseDeveloperExceptionPage** middleware component then calls the **Run** middleware component that is used to process every response. **Run** is not frequently used because it is a terminal piece of middleware, which means that it is the end of the pipeline. No middleware component added after the **Run** component will execute, because **Run** doesn't call into any other middleware components.

```
app.Run(async (context) =>
{
    var message = Configuration["Message"];
    await context.Response.WriteAsync(message);
});
```

By using the **context** object passed-in to the **Run** method, you can find out anything about the request through its **Request** object; the header information for instance. It will also have access to a **Response** object, which currently is used to print out a string.

Most middleware components will be added by calling a method beginning with **Use** on the **app** object, such as **app.UseDeveloperExceptionPage**.

As you can see, there are several middleware components available out of the box using the **app** object. You can add more middleware components by installing NuGet packages containing middleware.

Handling Exceptions

Let's have a look at how exception messages are handled by the pipeline. As previously mentioned the **app.UseDeveloperExceptionPage** middleware is in place to help the developer with any exceptions that might occur. To test this behavior, you can add a **throw** statement at the top of the **Run**-block and refresh the application in the browser.

1. Open the *Startup.cs* file and locate the **Run** middleware in the **Configure** method.
2. Add a generic **throw** statement that returns the string *Fake Exception!* to the **Run**-block.

```
app.Run(async (context) =>
{
    throw new Exception("Fake Exception!");
    var message = Configuration["Message"];
    await context.Response.WriteAsync(message);
});
```

3. If you haven't already started the application, press Ctrl+F5 to start it without debugging. Otherwise switch to the browser and refresh the application.
4. A pretty error message will be displayed. Note that this message only will be displayed when in development mode. On this page, you can read detailed information about the error, query strings, cookie information, and header content.

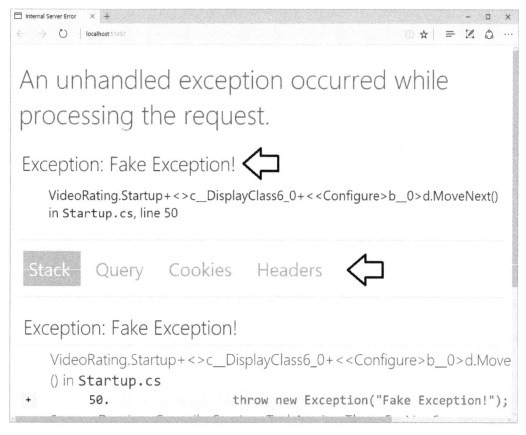

Now let's see what happens if you change the environment variable to *Production* and refresh the page.

1. Select **Project-*AspNetCorePublisherWebAPI* Properties** in the main menu.
2. Click on the **Debug** tab on the left side of the dialog.
3. Change the **ASPNETCORE_ENVIRONMENT** property to *Production*.
4. Save all files (Ctrl+Shift+S).
5. Refresh the application in the browser.
6. Now you will get an *HTTP 500 - Can't display this page* error, which is what a regular user would see. If you don't see this message, then you have to manually build the project with Ctrl+F5.

7. Switch back to Visual Studio and change back the **ASPNETCORE_ENVIRONMENT** property to *Development*.
8. Save all files.
9. Refresh the application in the browser; you should now be back to the pretty error page.

Now let's see what happens if we comment out the **app.UseDeveloperExceptionPage** middleware.

1. Open the *Setup.cs* file and locate the **Configure** method.
2. Comment out the call to the **app.UseDeveloperExceptionPage** middleware.
   //app.UseDeveloperExceptionPage();

3. Save the file.
4. Refresh the application in the browser.
5. The plain HTTP 500 error should be displayed because you no longer are loading the middleware that produces the pretty error message.
6. Uncomment the code again and save the file.
7. Refresh the browser one last time to make sure that the pretty error message is displayed.
8. Remove the **throw** statement from the **Run**-block and save the file.

You can use the **IHostingEnvironment** object, passed in through dependency injection, to find out information about the environment. Earlier you used the **IHostingEnvironment** object in an if-statement to determine if the development environment is used, and if so, display a pretty error page. You can also use it to find out the absolute path to the *wwwroot* directory in the project with the **WebRootPath** property.

Installing Postman

In this book, you will test the Web APIs you create using a Chrome tool called Postman, with which you can make calls to your Web APIs controller actions.

1. Navigate to www.getpostman.com/apps in your Chrome browser.
2. Select which version you want to install by clicking one of the install buttons.
3. When the download has completed, run the Postman installation file.
4. Follow the instructions.
5. Open Postman and pin it to the windows **Task** bar for easy access.

The image below shows key areas you will use in Postman.

1. In the **History** list, all previous requests are stored for easy access.
2. Click this drop-down button to select the desired HTTP Verb to use for the request. The most common ones are: Get, Put, Post, Patch, and Delete.
3. Here you enter the request URL.
4. Click the **Send** button to send the request to the specified URL with the settings made in the **Request** section.
5. Here, in the **Request** section, you make the necessary settings before sending the request, such as the request headers and body.
6. Here, in the **Response** area, the returned data and status code are displayed.

Setting Up ASP.NET MVC/Web API

The last thing you will do in this chapter is to set up the ASP.NET Core MVC middleware and add a simple controller to test that it works. This middleware is also used when creating Web API applications. With ASP.NET Core, the MVC and Web API controllers use the same middleware and services to handle requests.

Three things need to be added to the application to enable MVC. First you need to add the **Microsoft.AspNetCore.Mvc** NuGet package, then you need to add the MVC services, and lastly you need to add the MVC middleware.

Then you need to add a controller class with a **Get** action method that can be requested from the browser, or in this case the Postman application. You will learn more about other Web API action methods in upcoming chapters. For now, let's look at a simple example.

Adding the MVC NuGet Package

To add the **Microsoft.AspNetCore.Mvc** NuGet package, you can either use the NuGet Manager or type in the package name into the *.csproj* file manually.

The controller that you add must inherit from the **Controller** class to get access to base class functionality for controllers. It also must have a route, a path, defined to make its action methods accessible. You can define the path using the **[Route]** attribute, a Web API controller path that usually begins with *api/* followed by the controller's name, in this case *test*.

```
[Route("api/test")]
```

1. Right click on the project node in the Solution Explorer and select **Edit AspNetCorePublisherWebAPI.csproj**.
2. Locate the **ItemGroup** element in the file.
3. Change the package reference for **AspNetCore** to *1.1.2*.
4. Add a new **PackageReference** element and assign the MVC NuGet package name to its **Include** attribute.
5. Choose the version number with the **Version** attribute; the *1.1.3* version is used in this example.
   ```
   <ItemGroup>
       <PackageReference Include="Microsoft.AspNetCore.Mvc"
           Version="1.1.3" />
       ...
   </ItemGroup>
   ```

6. Save the file to install the NuGet package. You might have to restart Visual Studio for the changes to take effect.

7. You must add a controller that can respond to the HTTP requests coming in to the application pipeline. The convention is to add controller classes to a folder named *Controllers*. Right click on the project node and select **Add-New Folder** and name it *Controllers*.

8. Right click on the *Controllers* folder and select **Add-Class**.

9. Name the class **TestController** and click the **Add** button. Let the class inherit from the controller class and add a **[Route]** attribute to the class defining the route *api/test*.
```
[Route("api/test")]
public class TestController : Controller
{
}
```

10. Add a **using** statement to the **Microsoft.AspNetCore.Mvc** namespace.
```
using Microsoft.AspNetCore.Mvc;
```

11. Add a public method named **Get** that returns **IActionResult**, to the **TestController** class. Return the string *Hello, from the controller!* inside a call to the **Ok** method. The **Ok** method will return a *200 OK* result to the caller, with the text in the response body. Add the **[HttpGet]** attribute to the method to specify that it should respond to **Get** requests when called.
```
[HttpGet]
public IActionResult Get()
{
    return Ok("Hello, from the controller!");
}
```

12. Open the *Startup.cs* file and locate the **Configure** method.

13. Comment out the **app.Run** implementation and add the MVC middleware above the commented out code by calling the **app.UseMvc** method.
```
app.UseMvc();
//app.Run(async (context) =>
//{
//    var message = Configuration["Message"];
//    await context.Response.WriteAsync(message);
//});
```

14. Locate the **ConfigureServices** method in the **Startup** class.

15. Add the MVC services to the **services** collection at the top of the method. This will give ASP.NET everything it needs to run a MVC/Web API application.
```
public void ConfigureServices(IServiceCollection services)
{
    services.AddMvc();
}
```
16. Save the files and run the application. An empty browser should be displayed.
17. Copy the URL from the browser. This is the request URL you will use to call your application through IIS server using Postman.
18. Open the Postman application (see image below).
    a. Paste in the URL in Postman's URL field *http://localhost:55098/api/test* (replace the port number with the number used by your server).
    b. Select the **GET** verb in the drop-down to the left of the URL field.
    c. Click the **Send** button.
    d. The status code *200 OK* is returned by the **Ok** method you added to the **Get** action.
    e. *Hello, from the controller!* should be displayed in the Response section.

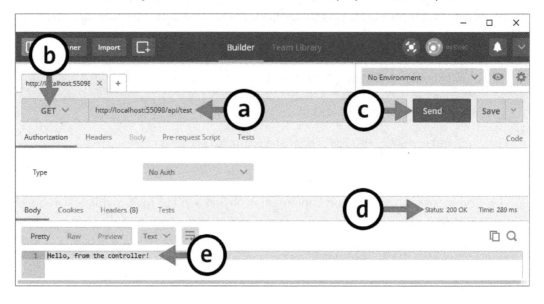

Complete code for the **TestController** class:

```
[Route("api/test")]
public class TestController : Controller
{
    [HttpGet]
    public IActionResult Get()
    {
        return Ok("Hello, from the controller!");
    }
}
```

Summary

In this chapter, you learned how to configure middleware in the **Configure** and **Configure-Services** methods of the **Startup** class.

The application now has several middleware components, including a developer error page and MVC. The MVC middleware can forward a request to an action method in a controller class to serve up content to the browser, or as in this case, return a response to an HTTP request.

You also used the Postman application to make a request to a **Get** action in your first Web API, returning a text response and a status code from the action method to Postman. In the next chapter, you will learn more about controllers.

3. Controllers

Introduction

In this chapter, you will learn about MVC, which is a popular design pattern for the user interface layer in applications, where *M* stands for Model, *V* stands for View, and *C* stands for Controller. In larger applications, MVC is typically combined with other design patterns, like data access and messaging patterns, to create a full application stack. This book will focus on the MVC fundamentals.

The controller is responsible for handling any HTTP requests that come to the application. It could be a user browsing to the */publishers* URL of the application. The controller's responsibility is then to gather and combine all the necessary data and package it in model objects, which act as data carriers to the views.

In an ASP.NET Core MVC application the model is sent to the view, which uses the data when it's rendered into HTML. The HTML is then sent back to the client browser as an HTML response. In an ASP.NET Core Web API application the view doesn't use HTML, Razor, or TagHelpers to render a user interface; instead it will return a resource, often in the form of JSON, to the calling application.

The MVC pattern creates a separation of concerns between the model, view, and controller. The sole responsibility of the controller is to handle the request and to build a model. The model's responsibility is to transport data and logic between the controller and the view, and the view is responsible for transforming that data into HTML or a resource.

For this to work, there must be a way to send HTTP requests to the correct controller. That is the purpose of ASP.NET MVC routing.

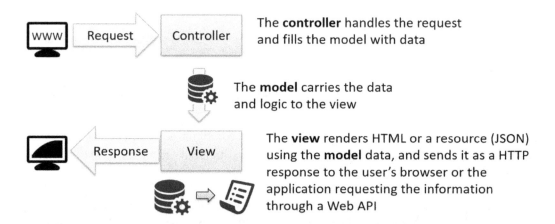

The **controller** handles the request and fills the model with data

The **model** carries the data and logic to the view

The **view** renders HTML or a resource (JSON) using the **model** data, and sends it as a HTTP response to the user's browser or the application requesting the information through a Web API

1. The user sends an HTTP request to the server by typing in a URL.
2. The controller on the server handles the request by fetching data and creating a model object.
3. The model object is sent to the view.
4. The view uses the data to render HTML or a resource (JSON).
5. The view is sent back to the user's browser in an HTTP response: HTML in the case of an ASP.NET Core MVC application, or as a resource (JSON) in the case of an ASP.NET Core Web API application.

Routing

The ASP.NET middleware you implemented in the previous chapter must be able to route incoming HTTP requests to a controller, since you are building an ASP.NET Core Web API application. The decision to send the request to a controller action is determined by the URL, and the configuration information you provide.

It is possible to define multiple routes. ASP.NET will evaluate them in the order they have been added. You can also combine convention-based routing with attribute routing if you need. Attribute routing is especially useful in Web API applications.

One way to provide the routing configuration is to use convention-based routing in the **Startup** class. With this type of configuration, you tell ASP.NET how to find the controller's name, action's name, and possibly parameter values in the URL. The controller is a C# class, and an action is a public method in a controller class. A parameter can be any value that can be represented as a string, such as an integer or a GUID.

The configuration can be done with a Lambda expression, as an inline method:

```
app.UseMvc(routes =>
{
    routes.MapRoute(
        name: "default",
        template: "{controller=Home}/{action=Index}/{id?}");
});
```

Or with an explicit method called from the **UseMvc** method inside the **Configure** method:

```
app.UseMvc(ConfigureRoutes);

...

private void ConfigureRoutes(IRouteBuilder routeBuildrer)
{
    routeBuildrer.MapRoute("Default",
        "{controller=Home}/{action=Index}/{Id?}");
}
```

ASP.NET looks at the route template to determine how to pull apart the URL. If the URL contains */Home* it will locate the **HomeController** class by convention, because the name begins with *Home*. If the URL contains */Home/Index*, ASP.NET will look for a public action method called **Index** inside the **HomeController** class. If the URL contains */Home/Index/ 123*, ASP.NET will look for a public action method called **Index** with an **Id** parameter inside the **HomeController** class. The *Id* is optional when defined with a question mark after its name. The controller and action names can also be omitted in the URL, because they have default values in the **Route** template.

Another way to implement routing is to use attribute routing, where you assign attributes to the controller class and its action methods. The metadata in those attributes tell ASP.NET when to call a specific controller and action.

Attribute routing requires a **using** statement to the **Microsoft.AspNetCore.Mvc** namespace.

```
[Route("[controller]/[action]")]
public class HomeController
{
}
```

When building an ASP.NET Core Web API, it's common to use specific names in the **[Route]** attribute, so that the route won't change. The reason an API route shouldn't change, even if the underlying class and action names change, is that a route can be viewed as a contract. If that contract is broken, the applications calling the API, to fetch or manipulate data, won't work anymore because they are calling endpoints (URLs) that no longer exist.

Instead of using a generic route as defined earlier, a specific route is often used in Web APIs. It is also common practice to prefix the route with *api* in Web API controllers. The action name part of the route is defined on each individual action using an HTTP verb attribute, for instance **[HttpGet]** when fetching data.

In this book, you will learn how to implement and call actions for the five most commonly used HTTP verbs: Get, Post, Put, Patch, and Delete.

In MVC applications, actions almost always return a view. In Web API applications, they usually return a response object that signals if the request was successful, or not, and passes along the actual data in the response body. In the example below, the status code *200 OK* will be returned to the calling application, along with the string *Hello, from the controller!* formatted as JSON in the request body.

Although action methods can return many different types of data, **IActionResult** is often used in Web APIs because it can return both a response status code and the actual data.

For MVC applications: [Route("[controller]/[action]")]

For Web APIs: [Route("api/home")]

```
[Route("api/home")]
public class HomeController : Controller
{
    [HttpGet]
    public IActionResult Get()
    {
        return Ok("Hello, from the controller!");
    }
}
```

HTTP Verbs and HTTP Attributes

When defining an action method in a Web API, you specify the URI to reach that action, by adding an HTTP attribute that contains the path to that action.

The HTTP attribute determines what the action is meant to do and what it will return in the response. There are five HTTP verbs that are commonly used in Web APIs: Get, Post, Put, Patch, and Delete. The verbs have corresponding attributes: **[HttpGet]**, **[HttpPost]**, **[HttpPut]**, **[HttpPatch]**, and **[HttpDelete]**.

HTTP Verb	Attribute	Sample URI	
GET	HttpGet	api/publisher	(list)
		api/publisher/1	(item with id 1)
POST	HttpPost	api/publisher	
PUT	HttpPut	api/publisher/1	
PATCH	HttpPatch	api/publisher/1	
DELETE	HttpDelete	api/publisher/1	

GET fetches a list of resources or a single resource by id. **POST** adds a new resource to the data source. **PUT** updates a whole resource. **PATCH** partially updates a resource, for instance one or more properties. **DELETE** removes a resource from the data source.

To determine what action to execute, the routing framework dissects the URL and matches it with the correct controller class (*api/publisher* for the **PublishersController** class). By convention, it then calls an action method based on the request verb used when calling the Web API. If the **GET** verb is used, an action method decorated with the **HttpGet** attribute will be called.

For instance, when you choose **GET** in the **Verb** drop-down in Postman, you, by extension, tell the routing framework to look for actions with the **HttpGet** attribute.

You can provide parameter values in the route, for instance an id to a specific resource. To do that you can add the parameter name in curly brackets *{id}* and then add a paramater with the same name to the action method.

Let's say that you want to enable users to delete a publisher from the data source. You could then add a **Delete** action with an integer parameter named **id** and specify in the route for that action that it should take a parameter named *id*.

41

You could specify a route template to use on the controller class with the **[Route]** attribute, for instance *api/publishers*, and the *{id}* parameter with the **HttpDelete** attribute.

You could then call *http://localhost:55098/api/publishers/2* from Postman to remove the publisher with id *2*. You would of course have to use the **DELETE** verb in Postman's dropdown when sending the request.

```
[Route("api/publishers")]
public class PublishersController : Controller
{
    [HttpDelete("{id}")]
    public IActionResult Delete(int id)
    {
        // Code to remove the resource
        return NoContent();
    }
}
```

Summary

In this chapter, you learned about the MVC (Model-View-Controller) design pattern; how the controller receives an HTTP request, gathers data from various sources, and creates a model, which then is processed into HTML or a resource (JSON) by the view.

In the next chapter, you will use model classes to transport data.

4. Models

Introduction
In this chapter, you will learn more about different types of model classes that you can use with Web APIs.

POCO Models
Using a model class, you can send objects with data and logic to the browser or the calling application. By convention, model classes should be stored in a folder called *Models*, but in larger applications it's not uncommon to store models in a separate project, which is referenced from the application. A model is a POCO (*Plain Old CLR Object* or *Plain Old C# Object*) class that can have attributes specifying how the receiver should behave when using it, such as checking the length of a string or if the data is required.

Let's add a **Message** model class that holds data about a message, such as a unique id and a text. Typically, you don't hardcode a model into a controller action; the objects are usually fetched from a data source such as a database (which you will do in a later chapter).

1. Right click on the project node in the Solution Explorer and select **Add-New Folder**.
2. Name the folder *Models*.
3. Right click on the *Models* folder and select **Add-Class**.
4. Name the class **Message** and click the **Add** button.
5. Add an **int** property called **Id**.
6. Add a **string** property called **Text** (Let's keep it simple for now).
    ```
    public class Message
    {
        public int Id { get; set; }
        public string Text { get; set; }
    }
    ```
7. Open the **TestController** class you added earlier.
8. Create an instance of the **Message** model class in the **Get** action and store it in a variable called **model**. Assign values to its properties when you instantiate it. You need to resolve the **Models** namespace to gain access to the **Message** class.
    ```
    var model = new Message { Id = 1, Text = "Message, from the Get
    action." };
    ```

9. Use the **Ok** response method to return the **model** object.
    ```
    return Ok(model);
    ```

10. Save the file and start the application. Open Postman and send a **Get** request to the *http://localhost:55098/api/test* URL (replace the port number with the one used by your web server).

11. When the response is returned, there are two things you should pay particular attention to: the status code and the returned JSON data (see image below).
    Status code: *200 OK*
    Data:
    ```
    {
        "id": 1,
        "text": "Message, from the Get action."
    }
    ```

The complete code for the **TestController** class:

```
[Route("api/test")]
public class TestController : Controller
{
    [HttpGet]
    public IActionResult Get()
    {
        var model = new Message { Id = 1,
            Text = "Message, from the Get action." };

        return Ok(model);
    }
}
```

Up until now, you have used the **Message** class as a model for the **Get** action. In simple solutions that might be fine, but in more complex Web API solutions, you need to use entity models and Data Transfer Objects (DTOs) to represent the data.

An entity model is typically used to define a table in a database, and a DTO is usually used to transform incoming request data into entity models, or entity data into response objects. This will be described in more detail when you learn how to fetch and manipulate data with Entity Framework Core.

Data Annotations

Data annotations are attributes you add to properties in a model, to enforce rules about them. You can specify that a field is required or must have a maximum number of characters or that it is a required value.

Many data annotations can be found in the **System.ComponentModel.DataAnnotations** namespace. You can specify one annotation per code line, or multiple annotations as a comma-separated list inside a set of square brackets.

You will use Data Annotations later in the book when you build the Publisher-Book Web APIs, using different data sources.

```
[Required]
[MaxLength(80)]
```

Or

```
[Required, MaxLength(80)]
```

The following code is just an example; don't add it to your code.

```
public class Message
{
    [Required]
    public int Id { get; set; }

    [Required, MaxLength(200)]
    public string Text { get; set; }
}
```

Below is a list of commonly used data annotations.

Name	Purpose
MinLength / MaxLength	Enforces length of strings
Range	Enforces min and max for numbers
RegularExpression	Makes a string match a pattern
Required	The model value is mandatory

Summary

In this chapter, you learned about different models that can be used with Web APIs, and how data annotations can be used to validate data

In the next section of the book, you will create a service component that fetches and updates in-memory data. The service is then used from the Web API controller actions when requests are made to the controller with Postman.

Part 2:
ASP.NET Core 1.1 Web API
Using In-Memory Data

5. Adding In-Memory Data Storage

Introduction

Now that you have a basic understanding of how a Web API works, it's time to introduce the first use case for an API that can fetch, add, update, and delete data using the previously mentioned **Get**, **Post**, **Put**, **Patch**, and **Delete** HTTP verbs.

During the remainder of this book you will create four Web API controllers for different purposes. The first two will work with in-memory data, and later with Entity Framework (EF) implementing the same interface and service as the in-memory service, to fetch data from a SQL Server database, and the remaining two will use a generic service to fetch data from a SQL Server database with EF.

The generic approach can be an excellent choice for code reuse when working with EF, since the code will work for any table.

All three scenarios will work with data relating to publishers and books. The interfaces, and service classes implementing them, will work with Data Transfer Objects (DTOs), the same classes that are used by the Web API actions to receive data.

Later, when working with EF entity classes, the DTOs will be transformed into entity objects when adding or updating data, and vice versa when returning data.

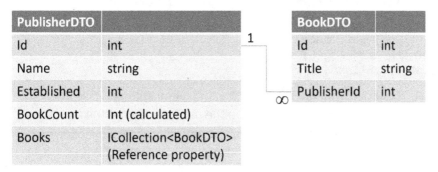

PublisherDTO	
Id	int
Name	string
Established	int
BookCount	Int (calculated)
Books	ICollection<BookDTO> (Reference property)

BookDTO	
Id	int
Title	string
PublisherId	int

As you can see in the image above, you will create two classes to begin with. The **Publisher-DTO** represents one publisher and the **BookDTO** represents one book. A publisher can have multiple books; which publisher a book belongs to is determined by the **PublisherId** property in the **BookDTO**. This means that a specific book can belong to only one publisher.

The data service that you will build uses these two DTOs to return and manipulate data in the data store. The action methods in the controllers will, however, use other DTOs to receive external data. The reason you use different DTOs is that all data isn't needed for all scenarios, and in the future, you might need to alter one scenario but not the others.

Let's start by creating the two main DTOs, **PublisherDTO** and **BookDTO**, since they will be used in the in-memory data collections.

Creating the Main DTOs

DTO classes are usually stored in the *Models* folder, but it can vary between projects. Some solutions even have separate projects for DTOs and entity classes.

1. If you haven't implemented the earlier examples, or if you have started a new project, then add a folder named *Models* to the project.
2. Right click on the *Models* folder and select **Add-Class**. Name the class **BookDTO** and click the **Add** button.
3. Add the public properties **Id (int)**, **Title (string)**, and **PublisherId (int)** to the class. The latter will determine which publisher owns the rights to a book.
   ```
   public int Id { get; set; }
   public string Title { get; set; }
   public int PublisherId { get; set; }
   ```
4. Add another class called **PublisherDTO** to the *Models* folder.
5. Add the public properties **Id (int)**, **Name (string)**,and **Established (int)** to the class.
   ```
   public int Id { get; set; }
   public string Name { get; set; }
   public int Established { get; set; }
   ```
6. Add a public **ICollection<BookDTO>** property and name it **Books**. This property will, if needed, contain the books related to the publisher. Note that an instance of the collection is created to avoid returning a **null** value if the collection isn't populated with data.
   ```
   public ICollection<BookDTO> Books { get; set; } =
   new List<BookDTO>();
   ```
7. Add a public property named **BookCount** that returns the number of books stored in the **Books** collection. It should only return a value, so don't add a **set-** block.
   ```
   public int BookCount { get { return Books.Count; } }
   ```

8. Save the classes.

The complete code for the **PublisherDTO** class:

```
public class PublisherDTO
{
    public int Id { get; set; }
    public string Name { get; set; }
    public int Established { get; set; }

    public int BookCount { get { return Books.Count; } }

    public ICollection<BookDTO> Books { get; set; } =
        new List<BookDTO>();
}
```

The complete code for the **BookDTO** class:

```
public class BookDTO
{
    public int Id { get; set; }
    public string Title { get; set; }
    public int PublisherId { get; set; }
}
```

Creating the In-Memory Data Collections

When building and testing a Web API, it is good to have reliable data that is consistent every time the application restarts. One way to achieve this to use in-memory data stored in collections that are filled when the application is started. In-memory data can easily be created using a static instance of the class containing the in-memory data.

Let's create the in-memory data collections in a class called **MockData** in a folder called *Data*.

The class will need two collections, one for each of the DTOs you just added, and a constructor that fills the collections with dummy data. To access the data easily, you will add a public static property called **Current** that returns an instance of the **MockData** class. Since the property is static, only one instance of the class will be created. You won't have to create any other instances of the class, the data and any changes will be preserved until the application is stopped.

Note that a **List** collection isn't thread safe, and should be used with caution in web applications; but this code is for experimental purposes, and the component will only ever be accessed by one user at a time.

1. Right click on the project node and select **Add-New Folder** and name it *Data*.
2. Right click on the *Data* folder and select **Add-Class**. Name the class **MockData** and click the **Add** button.
3. Add a **public static** property named **Current** of the **MockData** class type. Create an instance of the class when declaring the property.
   ```
   public static MockData Current { get; } = new MockData();
   ```
4. Add the two **List** collection properties for the **PublisherDTO** and the **BookDTO**; name them **Publishers** and **Books** respectively. To get access to the DTOs, you will have to resolve their namespace, or manually add a **using** statement to the **Models** namespace.
   ```
   public List<PublisherDTO> Publishers { get; set; }
   public List<BookDTO> Books { get; set; }
   ```
5. Add a constructor to the class.
   ```
   public MockData()
   {
   }
   ```
6. Add a couple of publishers to the **Publishers** collection.
   ```
   Publishers = new List<PublisherDTO>
   {
       new PublisherDTO {  Id = 1, Established = 1921,
           Name = "Publishing House 1" },
       new PublisherDTO {  Id = 2, Established = 1888,
           Name = "Publishing House 2" }
   };
   ```
7. Add a few books to the **Books** collection, referencing publisher ids in the **Publishers** collection.
   ```
   Books = new List<BookDTO>
   {
       new BookDTO { Id = 1, PublisherId = 2, Title = "Book 1" },
       new BookDTO { Id = 2, PublisherId = 1, Title = "Book 2" },
       new BookDTO { Id = 3, PublisherId = 2, Title = "Book 3" },
       new BookDTO { Id = 4, PublisherId = 1, Title = "Book 4" }
   };
   ```
8. Save all files.

The complete code for the **MockData** class:

```
public class MockData
{
    // Create static instance of the MockData class
    public static MockData Current { get; } = new MockData();
    public List<PublisherDTO> Publishers { get; set; }
    public List<BookDTO> Books { get; set; }

    public MockData()
    {
        Publishers = new List<PublisherDTO>
        {
            new PublisherDTO {  Id = 1, Established = 1921,
                Name = "Publishing House 1" },
            new PublisherDTO {  Id = 2, Established = 1888,
                Name = "Publishing House 2" }
        };

        Books = new List<BookDTO>
        {
            new BookDTO { Id = 1, PublisherId = 2, Title = "Book 1" },
            new BookDTO { Id = 2, PublisherId = 1, Title = "Book 2" },
            new BookDTO { Id = 3, PublisherId = 2, Title = "Book 3" },
            new BookDTO { Id = 4, PublisherId = 1, Title = "Book 4" }
        };
    }
}
```

Summary

In this chapter, you created two DTO classes and used them in mock in-memory data collections.

In the next chapter, you will fetch the in-memory data from a service that you add.

6. Adding an In-Memory Data Service

Introduction

Instead of using one specific source to fetch data, you can use services to fetch data from different sources, depending on the circumstance. This mean that you, through the use of configuration, can use different data sources according to the need at hand.

You might want to fetch data from a JSON file when building the service, and later switch to another implementation of that service, to work with data from a database.

To achieve this, you create an interface that the service classes implement, and then use that interface when serving up the instances. Because the service classes implement the same interface, instances from them are interchangeable.

To get access to the services from the **Configure** method in the **Startup** class, or any other constructor, model, or view, you must use dependency injection. That is, pass in the interface as a parameter to the method.

You must register the service interface, and the desired service class, with the **services** collection in the **ConfgureServices** method, in the **Startup** class. This determines which class will be used to create the instance, when dependency injection is used to pass in an instance of a class implementing the interface.

In the next chapter, you will inject a service class into the constructor of a controller called **PublishersController**, but you can also inject regular POCO classes into a constructor, model, or view, using dependency injection.

You might wonder how the **IApplicationBuilder** parameter gets populated in the **Configure** method in the **Startup** class, when no configuration has been added for it in the **ConfigureServices** method. The answer is that certain service objects will be served up for interfaces automatically by ASP.NET; one of those interfaces is the **IApplicationBuilder**. Another is the **IHostingEnvironment** service, which handles different environments, such as development, staging, and production.

When adding a service to the service collection, you can choose between several **Add** methods. Here's a rundown of the most commonly used.

Singleton creates a single instance that is used throughout the application. It creates the instance when the first dependency-injected object is created.

Scoped services are lifetime services, created once per request within the scope. It is equivalent to **Singleton** in the current scope. In other words, the same instance is reused within the same HTTP request.

Transient services are created each time they are requested and won't be reused. This lifetime works best for lightweight, stateless services.

Adding the BookstoreMockRepository Data Service

Hardcoding data in a controller is not good practice, because the controller will be hard, if not impossible, to test, and will contain a lot of code. Instead you want to take advantage of dependency injection to make data available. You typically do this by injecting the service into the constructor and save it in a private class-level field.

One big benefit of implementing a service is that its interface can be used to implement different components. In this book, you will implement one for mock in-memory data and one for a SQL Server database, using the same service interface.

In this section, you will add a **BookstoreMockRepository** component that implements an interface called **IBookstoreRepository**, and uses the data in the static **MockData** class instance.

To begin with, the interface will only define one method called **GetPublishers**, which will return a **IEnumerable<PublisherDTO>** collection. You will add more methods to the interface and service as you progress through the book.

1. Add a folder called *Services* to the project folder.
2. Right click on the *Services* folder and select **Add-New Item**.
3. Select the **Interface** template, name it **IBookstoreRepository**, and click the **Add** button.
4. Add the **public** access modifier to the interface to make it publicly available.
   ```
   public interface IBookstoreRepository
   {
   }
   ```

5. Add a method called **GetPublishers** that returns a **GetPublisherDTO** collection.
   ```
   IEnumerable<PublisherDTO> GetPublishers();
   ```

6. Right click on the *Services* folder and select **Add-Class**.

7. Name the class **BookstoreMockRepository** and click the **Add** button.

8. Implement the **IBookstoreRepository** interface in the class. Add the interface name and point to the red squiggly line, then click on the lightbulb button and select **Implement Interface**.
   ```
   public class BookstoreMockRepository : IBookstoreRepository
   {
       public IEnumerable<PublisherDTO> GetPublishers()
       {
           throw new NotImplementedException();
       }
   }
   ```

9. Remove the **throw** statement in the **GetPublishers** method and return the **Publishers** collection from the **MockData** class, using the class's **Current** property.
   ```
   public IEnumerable<PublisherDTO> GetPublishers()
   {
       return MockData.Current.Publishers;
   }
   ```

10. Open the **Startup** class.

11. Now that the service is complete, you must add it to the **services** collection in the **Startup** class's **ConfigureServices** method. Register the **IBookstoreRepository** interface to create instances of the **BookstoreMockRepository** using the **AddScoped** method; this will ensure that one object is created for each HTTP request. The HTTP request can then flow through many services and share the same instance of the **MockData** class.
    ```
    services.AddScoped(typeof(IBookstoreRepository),
        typeof(BookstoreMockRepository));
    ```

The code for the **IBookstoreRepository** interface, so far:

```
public interface IBookstoreRepository
{
    IEnumerable<PublisherDTO> GetPublishers();
}
```

The code for the **BookstoreMockRepository** class, so far:

```
public class BookstoreMockRepository : IBookstoreRepository
{
    public IEnumerable<PublisherDTO> GetPublishers()
    {
        return MockData.Current.Publishers;
    }
}
```

The code for the **ConfigureServices** method, so far:

```
public void ConfigureServices(IServiceCollection services)
{
    services.AddMvc();

    services.AddScoped(typeof(IBookstoreRepository),
        typeof(BookstoreMockRepository));
}
```

Summary

In this chapter, you created and registered a service to make it available through dependency injection in other parts of the application.

In the next chapter, you will use this service from the **Get** action in the **Publishers-Controller** class that you will add. You will also add methods to the service and use them in the controller.

7. Adding the Publishers Controller

Introduction

In this chapter, you will implement the **PublishersController** class, the first two controller classes dealing with publishers and books.

To fetch and manipulate in-memory data (in the **MockData** class), you will add methods to the **IBookstoreRepository** interface and implement them in the **BookstoreRepository** service. You will then use those methods in the **PublishersController** to handle requests from the consumer, which in this case is Postman.

The first action you will add to the **Publishers** controller is a **Get** action that returns a list of all publishers in the data store. You will call the **GetPublishers** method you created in the service in the previous chapter to fetch the publishers.

Then you will add methods, one at a time for: fetching a publisher (**Get**), adding a new publisher (**Post**), modifying an existing publisher (**Put** and **Patch**), and removing a publisher (**Delete**). You will call the actions, using Postman as you add them to the controller.

Status Codes

When returning the response to the consumer, it's important to specify the correct status code. If you always use status *200 OK* for instance, the consuming application will think that your Web API always succeeds, even if an error occurs. You should therefore make sure that each Web API action returns a status code reflecting the outcome.

In a **Post** action where a new resource has been created successfully, a status code of *201 Created* would be an excellent choice, and for a **Delete** request a *204 No Content* would be the best choice.

If an error occurs, the choice of status code depends on whether the error was instigated on the client or on the server. If a client for instance sends badly formatted JSON that can't be parsed, a reasonable status code would be *400 Bad Request*. If the error originated on the server, however, the status code should be *500 Internal Server Error*.

You will use the following response methods in the ASP.NET Core MVC framework to return correct status codes from your controller actions: **Ok** (*200 OK*), **NoContent** (*204 No Content*), **BadRequest** (*400 Bad Request*), and **NotFound** (*404 Not Found*).

The following image shows where the status code and response data (body) is displayed in Postman.

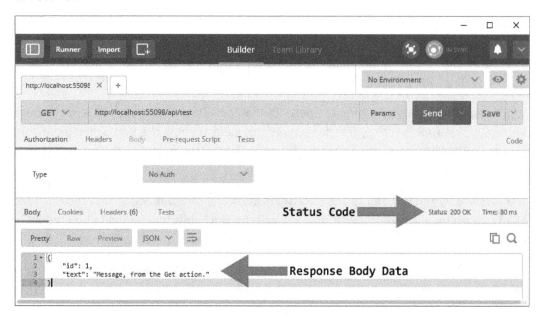

The most common response status codes used with Web APIs are listed in the tables below. Several of them have corresponding methods in ASP.NET Core that can be used in action methods to send the correct status code back to the consumer.

Success Status Codes

Status Code	Description
200 OK	The get request was successful.
201 Created	A new resource was successfully created.
204 No Content	A successful request that shouldn't return anything, such as deleting a resource.

Server Error Status Codes

Status Code	Description
500 Internal Server Error	The error occurred on the server and the consumer, for instance a client side web app; can't do anything about it.

Client Error Status Codes

Status Code	Description
400 Bad Request	There's something wrong with the client's request; it could be non-parsable JSON.
401 Unauthorized	No, or invalid, authentication was provided.
403 Forbidden	Successful authentication, but the user does not have access to the requested resource.
404 Not Found	The requested resource does not exist.
409 Conflict	A conflict occurred. Could be between two simultaneous updates.

Adding the Publishers Controller

As you have seen in previous examples, the controller receives the HTTP requests from the routing framework and responds to those requests. Now, you will create the **PublishersController** class, one of two controllers that you will work with in this part of the book.

This controller will handle all requests pertaining to fetching, creating, updating, and deleting publisher resources. Later you will create a similar controller for book resources.

To get access to the in-memory data, you will use dependency injection to inject an instance of the **BookstoreMockRepository** service into the constructor, using the **IBookstoreRepository** interface as the injected type. Store the instance in a class-level variable to make it accessible throughout the controller.

1. Add a class called **PublishersController** to the *Controllers* folder.
2. Inherit the **Controller** class to get access to basic controller functionality. You must resolve or add a **using** statement to the **Microsoft.AspNetCore.Mvc** namespace.
   ```
   public class PublishersController : Controller
   {
   }
   ```
3. Add attribute routing to *api/publishers* above the class.
   ```
   [Route("api/publishers")]
   ```
4. Add a constructor to the class and inject the **IBookstoreRepository** interface as its dependency-injected type. When the controller is created an instance of the **BookstoreMockRepository** service will be injected through the interface. You need to add a **using** statement to the **Services** namespace.

```
public PublishersController(IBookstoreRepository rep)
{
}
```

5. Add a class-level variable to hold the injected instance.
    ```
    IBookstoreRepository _rep;
    ```

6. Assign the injected instance to the class-level variable inside the constructor.
    ```
    _rep = rep;
    ```

7. Save the controller.

The **PublishersController** class, so far:

```
[Route("api/publishers")]
public class PublishersController : Controller
{
    IBookstoreRepository _rep;
    public PublishersController(IBookstoreRepository rep)
    {
        _rep = rep;
    }
}
```

Get a List of Publishers (GET)

Now you will fetch all publishers from the in-memory data and return them to the consumer using the **Ok** method, which will generate a *200 OK* response status code and send the publishers with the response body data.

You don't have to do any checks before returning the publisher collection because if the collection hasn't been instantiated a *204 No Content* status code will be returned, and if it has been instantiated but is empty a *200 OK* will be returned along with an empty list.

Let's add the action method that will return the publishers from the in-memory data.

1. Add a public method called **Get** to the controller class. The method should return **IActionResult.** .
    ```
    public IActionResult Get()
    {
    }
    ```

2. Decorate the method with the **[HttpGet]** attribute. You don't have to add anything to the attribute since it doesn't have any parameters.

```
[HttpGet]
public IActionResult Get()
```

3. Use the **Ok** response method to return the list of publishers you fetch by calling the **GetPublishers** method in the service using the **_rep** class-level variable.
```
return Ok(_rep.GetPublishers());
```

4. Run the application without debugging (Ctrl+F5) and copy the URL.

5. Open Postman and paste in the URL in the URL field and add the */api/publishers* URI: *http://localhost:55098/api/publishers* (the port number might be different for your server).

6. Make sure that **GET** is selected in the drop-down.

7. Click the **Send** button.

8. The response should contain the publishers you added to the **MockData** class earlier and display a *200 OK* status code (see image below).

```
[
    {
        "id": 1,
        "name": "Publishing House 1",
        "established": 1921,
        "bookCount": 0,
        "books": []
    },
    {
        "id": 2,
        "name": "Publishing House 2",
        "established": 1888,
        "bookCount": 0,
        "books": []
    }
]
```

9. Close the browser to stop the application.

The complete code for the **Get** action:

```
[HttpGet]
public IActionResult Get()
{
    return Ok(_rep.GetPublishers());
}
```

This image shows the response for a successful get in Postman.

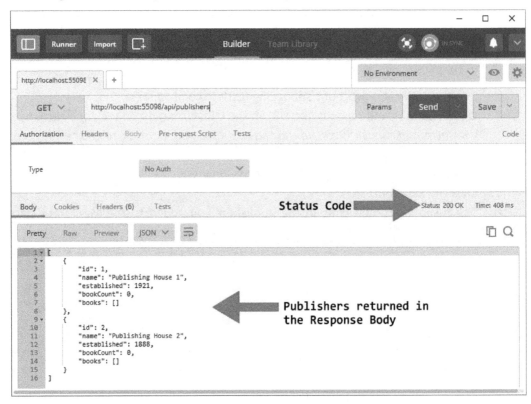

1. Open the **MockData** class and comment out the **Publishers** collection in the constructor.

```
//Publishers = new List<PublisherDTO>()
//{
//    new PublisherDTO {  Id = 1, Established = 1921,
//        Name = "Publishing House 1" },
//    new PublisherDTO {  Id = 2, Established = 1888,
//        Name = "Publishing House 2" }
//};
```

2. Run the application again and send the same request from Postman. A *204 No Content* status code should be returned and the response body should be empty (see image below).

3. Close the browser to stop the application.

This image shows the response for a successful get where the **Publishers** collection hasn't been instantiated.

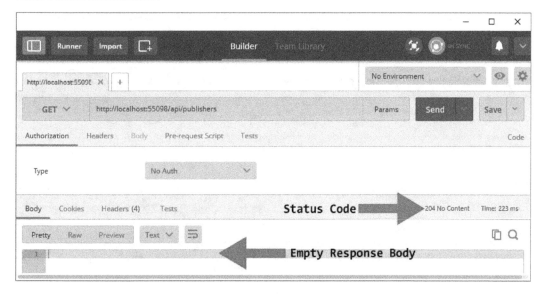

1. Uncomment the first line of the commented-out code and add parentheses and a semicolon at the end.
    ```
    Publishers = new List<PublisherDTO>();
    ```

2. Run the application again and send the same request from Postman. A *200 OK* status code should be returned and the response body should contain an empty collection (see image below).

3. Close the browser to stop the application.

4. Uncomment the rest of the code in the **MockData** class's constructor to once again return publishers.
    ```
    Publishers = new List<PublisherDTO>
    {
        new PublisherDTO {  Id = 1, Established = 1921,
            Name = "Publishing House 1" },
        new PublisherDTO {  Id = 2, Established = 1888,
            Name = "Publishing House 2" }
    };
    ```

5. Save all files.

This image shows the response for a successful get where the **Publishers** collection has been instantiated and is empty.

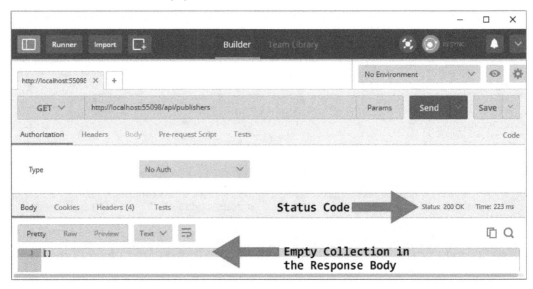

Get a Single Publisher (GET)

Now that you have created an action to fetch a list of publishers from the in-memory data, it's time to modify the service interface and class. You will add a method called **GetPublisher** that fetches a single publisher with or without its related books. The method will take two parameters: **publisherId (int)** and **includeBooks (bool)**. The first parameter identifies the desired publisher and the second parameter determines if the books related to the publisher also should be returned.

Then you will call the newly added method from a second **Get** action in the **Publishers-Controller** class. The URI for this action should define a parameter called *id* that also is added as an **int** parameter called **id** to the **Get** action method.

Because this action later will be called from another action method, you should add a **Name** parameter to the **HttpGet** attribute and assign the name *GetPublisher* to it.

```
[HttpGet("{id}", Name ="GetPublisher")]
public IActionResult Get(int id, bool includeBooks = false)
```

A URL to reach this action could look like this: *http://localhost:55098/api/publishers/5*, where the number after the last slash is the id for the desired publisher; it will match *{id}* in the URI and the **id** parameter in the method.

Adding the GetPublisher Method to the Service

1. Open the **IBookstoreRepository** interface.
2. Add a method definition for a method called **GetPublisher** that takes two parameters: **publisherId (int)** and **includeBooks (bool)**. The latter parameter should have a default value of **false**, and the method should return a **PublisherDTO** instance.
    ```
    PublisherDTO GetPublisher(int publisherId, bool includeBooks =
    false);
    ```
3. Open the **BookstoreMockRepository** service class.
4. Add the new method from the interface. You can right click on the squiggly line to add it, like you have done before.
    ```
    public PublisherDTO GetPublisher(int publisherId, bool
    includeBooks = false) {
        throw new NotImplementedException();
    }
    ```
5. Delete the **throw** statement.
6. Use the **FirstOrDefault** LINQ method to fetch the publisher from the **MockData** class that matches the **publisherId** parameter value and store it in a variable called **publisher**.
    ```
    var publisher = MockData.Current.Publishers.FirstOrDefault(p =>
    p.Id.Equals(publisherId));
    ```
7. To only include the books related to the publisher, when the **includeBooks** parameter is **true**, you must add an if-block that only is executed when the **publisher** variable is not **null** and the **includeBooks** parameter is **true**. Inside the if-block, you fetch the books from the **MockData** class and assign them to the **Books** property of the **publisher** instance. Use the **Where** LINQ method to fetch the books where the **publisherId** parameter matches publisher ids in the **Books** collection.
    ```
    if (includeBooks && publisher != null)
    {
        publisher.Books = MockData.Current.Books.Where(b =>
            b.PublisherId.Equals(publisherId)).ToList();
    }
    ```

8. Return the value stored in the **publisher** variable.

```
return publisher;
```

The code in the **IBookstoreRepository** interface, so far:

```
public interface IBookstoreRepository
{
    IEnumerable<PublisherDTO> GetPublishers();
    PublisherDTO GetPublisher(int publisherId,
        bool includeBooks = false);
}
```

The complete code in the **GetPublisher** method:

```
public PublisherDTO GetPublisher(int publisherId, bool includeBooks =
false)
{
    var publisher = MockData.Current.Publishers.FirstOrDefault(p =>
        p.Id.Equals(publisherId));

    if (includeBooks && publisher != null)
    {
        publisher.Books = MockData.Current.Books.Where(b =>
            b.PublisherId.Equals(publisherId)).ToList();
    }

    return publisher;
}
```

Calling the GetPublisher Method from the Controller

This method should fetch one publisher from the **MockData** class and return it with or without its corresponding books, depending on the value in the **includeBooks** parameter.

It should take two parameters: **id (int)**, which is the id of the publisher to fetch, and **includeBooks (bool)**, which determines if the books related to a publisher should be returned.

If no publisher matches the passed-in id, then a *404 Not Found* status code should be returned using the **NotFound** method.

The **[HttpGet]** attribute should define a parameter called *id* inside curly brackets *{id}* and be given the name *GetPublisher* using the **Name** property. The *{id}* parameter should match a parameter called **id (int)** in the method definition.

```
[HttpGet("{id}", Name ="GetPublisher")]
public IActionResult Get(int id, bool includeBooks = false)
```

To specify a value for the **includeBooks** parameter, you tag on a question mark (?) followed by the parameter name and value to the URL when calling the action. If you leave it out the default value (**false**) will be used.

http://localhost:55098/api/publishers/5?includeBooks=true

1. Open the **PublishersController** class.
2. Add an **[HttpGet]** below the previously added **Get** method and add the *{id}* parameter and the **Name** property to it.
   ```
   [HttpGet("{id}", Name ="GetPublisher")]
   ```

3. Add a method called **Get** that returns **IActionResult** and takes two parameters: **id (int)** and **includeBooks (bool)** that has the default value **false**.
   ```
   public IActionResult Get(int id, bool includeBooks = false)
   {
   }
   ```

4. Use the **GetPublisher** method that you added to the service to fetch the publisher matching the **id** and **includeBooks** parameter values passed-in to the action method through the URI. You reach the service by using the **_rep** variable. Store the result in a variable called **publisher**.
   ```
   var publisher = _rep.GetPublisher(id, includeBooks);
   ```

5. Return the publisher with the **Ok** method to signal that the publisher was fetched correctly.
   ```
   return Ok(publisher);
   ```

6. Run the application (F5).
7. Open Postman and enter the URL to a non-existing publisher (use a publisher id that does not exist in the **MockData** class) and click the **Send** button. This should return an empty response body and a status code of *204 No Content*, which is the wrong status code; it should be *404 Not Found* since the publisher doesn't exist (see image below).
   http://localhost:55098/api/publishers/5

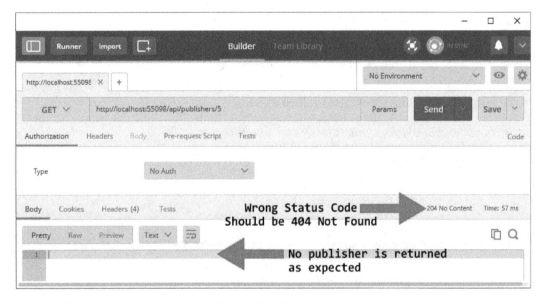

8. Close the browser to stop the application.
9. Open the **PublishersController** class and locate the **Get** action you just added.
10. Add an if-statement that checks if the **publisher** variable is **null** between the two existing code lines. Return *404 Not Found*, using the **NotFound** method, if the **publisher** variable is **null**.

    ```
    if (publisher == null) return NotFound();
    ```

11. Start the application and run the same request again. Now the response status code should be *404 Not Found* (see image below).

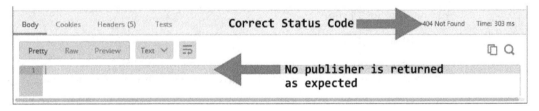

12. Now request the first publisher in your **MockData** class from Postman (one that exists). Add the **includeBooks** parameter and set its value to **false**. Then click the **Send** button.

    *http://localhost:55098/api/publishers/1?includeBooks=**false***

    Note that the **Books** collection is empty in the response (see image below).

```
{
    "id": 1,
    "name": "Publishing House 1",
    "established": 1921,
    "bookCount": 0,
    "books": []
}
```

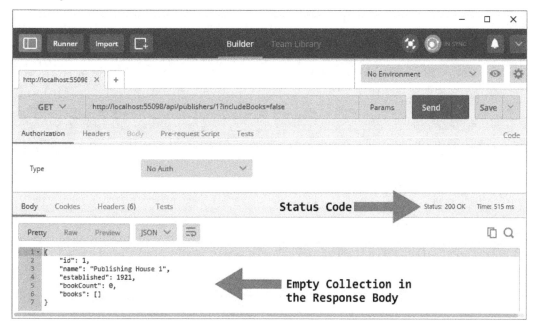

13. Change the **includeBooks** parameter to **true** and send the request again.
    http://localhost:55098/api/publishers/1?includeBooks=true
    Note that the **Books** collection now contains books in the response (see image below).
    ```
    {
        "id": 1,
        "name": "Publishing House 1",
        "established": 1921,
        "bookCount": 2,
        "books": [
            {
                "id": 2,
                "title": "Book 2",
                "publisherId": 1
    ```

```
        },
        {
            "id": 4,
            "title": "Book 4",
            "publisherId": 1
        }
    ]
}
```

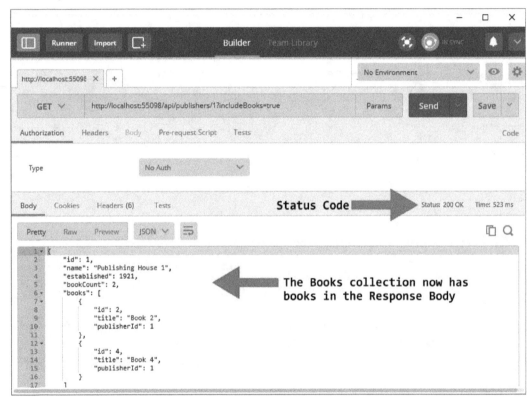

14. Close the browser to stop the application.

*Note: Because you are using a **static** collection in the **MockData** class, the books will be assigned to the publisher whether you set the **includeBooks** parameter to **false** or **true** once a publisher has been fetched with books. You must close the browser and restart the application to reset the data. This will not be the case when working with a database.*

The complete code for the **Get** action in the **PublishersController** class:

```
[HttpGet("{id}", Name = "GetPublisher")]
public IActionResult Get(int id, bool includeBooks = false)
{
    var publisher = _rep.GetPublisher(id, includeBooks);

    if (publisher == null) return NotFound();

    return Ok(publisher);
}
```

Add Status Code Pages

If you run the application and navigate to a URL for a non-existing publisher in the browser, an empty page is displayed. You must open the browser's Developer Tools (F12) to see the *404 Not Found* error.

To change this behavior for the browser, you can add a middleware component that displays the status code in the browser.

1. Run the application (F5) and navigate to a non-existing publisher in the URL field. An empty page is displayed in the browser.
   http://localhost:55098/api/publishers/5

2. Open the Developer Tools (F12) and show the errors. Stop the application.

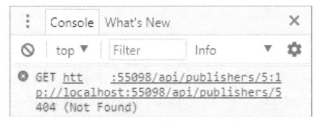

3. Open the **Startup** class and locate the **Configure** method.
4. Add a call to the **UseStatusCodePages** method above the **UseMvc** method call.
   `app.UseStatusCodePages();`

5. Save the file and start the application (F5) and navigate to the same URL as before. Now the status code should be displayed in the browser window.

6. Close the browser to stop the application.
7. Comment out the the **UseStatusCodePages** method call.

Add a Publisher (POST)

Now that you know how to fetch data, it's time to learn how to add data. To add data, you use the HTTP **Post** verb in Postman, or from a client application.

The **Post** method will receive the data from the request body. To collect that data in the action method, you use the **[FromBody]** attribute on the parameter receiving the data. ASP.NET will then automatically match the properties in the incoming data with properties in the **publisher** object.

```
public IActionResult Post([FromBody] PublisherCreateDTO publisher)
```

When receiving data for an update, the object created for the parameter won't have an id since it doesn't exist in the in-memory data yet. It is therefore common to use a separate DTO class to represent the create object. You will add a new class to the *Models* folder for a DTO class called **PublisherCreateDTO**. The class will have two properties: **Name (string)** and **Established (int)**.

To help the client determine how to use the properties and report errors for certain scenarios, you use data annotation attributes on properties where needed. Let's say for instance that the **Name** property is a required field and must have a maximum length of 50 characters; to enforce this behavior you could add the **[Required]** and **[MaxLength]** attributes to it. To gain access to the data annotation attributes, you have to add a **using** statement to the **System.ComponentModel.DataAnnotations** namespace.

There are certain checks that you need to do in the **Post** action to ensure that the correct data and status code are returned from the action.

- Check if the DTO is **null**, and if so, return a bad request status code.

- Add custom error checks if necessary. You can for instance check that the **Estab-lished** property contains a value greater than or equal to the year of the first known publisher (1534). If it is, then add an error to the **ModelState** object with the **AddModelError** method.

- After adding the custom validation, you check the **ModelState** object to see if any model state errors exist and return a bad request along with the model state object.

If the validation succeeds, you create a new instance of the **PublisherDTO** and assign property values from the **PublisherCreateDTO** instance. You then add the **PublisherDTO** to the in-memory data.

To be able to add the publisher to the **Publishers** collection, you need to add a method called **AddPublisher** to the service interface and the service class. The method should take the newly created **PublisherDTO** object as its only parameter.

The **AddPublisher** method then adds the publisher object to the **Publishers** collection in the **MockData** class by calling the **Add** method on the collection.

When the publisher has been saved, you redirect to the **GetPublisher** route (the latest **Get** action you added) by calling the **CreateAtRoute** method with the route name, the **Get** action parameters, and the added publisher object. If you recall, you added a name to the **Get** action with the **[HttpGet]** attribute for this reason.

Adding the PublisherCreateDTO Class

Since the publisher doesn't exist in the **Publishers** collection yet, it hasn't got an id. It would therefore be pointless to have an **Id** property in the DTO class. To separate the different scenarios of adding and updating resources from fetching data, it is common practice to use separate DTOs for these three scenarios. The DTOs for updating and adding resources will have the same properties in this project, but in a real-world scenario, they might not.

1. Add a class called **PublisherCreateDTO** to the *Models* folder.
2. Add two properties to the class: **Name** (**string**) and **Established** (**int**).
3. Add two data annotations to the **Name** property: **MaxLength(50)** and **Required**, with its **ErrorMessage** property set to *You must enter a name*.
   ```
   [Required(ErrorMessage = "You must enter a name.")]
   [MaxLength(50)]
   ```

4. Save the class.

The complete code for the **PublisherCreateDTO** class:

```
public class PublisherCreateDTO
{
    [Required(ErrorMessage = "You must enter a name.")]
    [MaxLength(50)]
    public string Name { get; set; }
    public int Established { get; set; }
}
```

Adding the AddPublisher Method to the Service

1. Open the **IBookstoreRepository** interface.
2. Add a method definition for a method named **AddPublisher** that takes a **PublisherDTO** instance as a parameter and doesn't return anything.
    ```
    void AddPublisher(PublisherDTO publisher);
    ```

3. Open the **BookstoreMockRepository** service class.
4. Add the **AddPublisher** method from the interface.
    ```
    public void AddPublisher(PublisherDTO publisher)
    {
        throw new NotImplementedException();
    }
    ```

5. Remove the **throw** statement.
6. Because the collections in the **MockData** class can't generate ids automatically, like a database, you must manually create a new id for the publisher. You can do this by calling the **Max** LINQ method on the collection and increment the value by one. Assign the new id to the passed-in publisher object. Note that you do this for demo purposes only.
    ```
    var id = GetPublishers().Max(m => m.Id) + 1;
    publisher.Id = id;
    ```

7. Add the publisher object to the **Publishers** collection.
    ```
    MockData.Current.Publishers.Add(publisher);
    ```

8. Save all files.

The complete code for the **AddPublisher** method:

```
public void AddPublisher(PublisherDTO publisher)
{
```

```
        // For Demo purposes only: Get next id
        var id = GetPublishers().Max(m => m.Id) + 1;
        publisher.Id = id;
        MockData.Current.Publishers.Add(publisher);
}
```

Adding the Save Method to the Service

When working with static data in collections, it's not necessary to explicitly save the data with a **Save** method. But when working with Entity Framework later, you will need a **Save** method. To keep the interface and the controller the same for both scenarios, you will add it now and have it return **true**.

1. Open the **IBookstoreRepository** interface.
2. Add a method definition for a parameterless method named **Save** that returns **bool**.
    ```
    bool Save();
    ```
3. Open the **BookstoreMockRepository** service class.
4. Add the **Save** method from the interface.
    ```
    public bool Save()
    {
        throw new NotImplementedException();
    }
    ```
5. Remove the **throw** statement and return **true**.
6. Save the files.

The complete code for the **Save** method:

```
public bool Save()
{
    return true;
}
```

The code in the **IBookstoreRepository** interface, so far:

```
public interface IBookstoreRepository
{
    IEnumerable<PublisherDTO> GetPublishers();
    PublisherDTO GetPublisher(int publisherId,
        bool includeBooks = false);
    void AddPublisher(PublisherDTO publisher);
    bool Save();
}
```

Adding the Post Action to the PublishersController Class

1. Open the **PublishersController** class.
2. Add an **[HttpPost]** attribute without parameters below the previously added **Get** methods.
3. Add a public method called **Post** that returns **IActionResult** and takes a parameter of type **PublisherCreateDTO** named **publisher** that is decorated with the **[FromBody]** attribute. The attribute ensures that the object is assigned data from the request body sent from the client, which in this case will be Postman.

   ```
   [HttpPost]
   public IActionResult Post([FromBody] PublisherCreateDTO publisher)
   { ... }
   ```

4. The first check you must add to the action is to see if the passed-in object is **null**, and if so, return *400 Bad Request*.

   ```
   if (publisher == null) return BadRequest();
   ```

5. Although not strictly necessary, you will add a custom check to see if the year the publishing house was established is earlier than 1534, the year when the first known publishing house was established. Check if the value in the **Established** property is less than 1534 and add a **ModelState** error if it is.

   ```
   if (publisher.Established < 1534)
       ModelState.AddModelError("Established",
           "The first publishing house was founded in 1534.");
   ```

6. Return *400 Bad Request* if the model state is invalid.

   ```
   if (!ModelState.IsValid) return BadRequest(ModelState);
   ```

7. Create an instance of the **PublisherDTO** class called **publisherToAdd** and assign the values from the **publisher** parameter. This is a crude way of mapping from one type to another. In a later chapter, you will use AutoMapper for this purpose.

   ```
   var publisherToAdd = new PublisherDTO {
       Established = publisher.Established, Name = publisher.Name };
   ```

8. Add the publisher object in the **publisherToAdd** variable to the **Publishers** collection in the **MockData** class by calling the **AddPublisher** method you just added to the repository service. Call the **Save** method. Even though it isn't necessary for this scenario, it will enable you to switch to an Entity Framework service later without modifying the controller.

   ```
   _rep.AddPublisher(publisherToAdd);
   _rep.Save();
   ```

9. The last bit of code you need to add is a call to the **GetPublisher** action using the **CreatedAtRoute** method. You call an existing action to reuse its code. The first parameter is the name of the action to call, the second is an anonymous object containing values for the **Get** action's parameters, and the last parameter is the added source object (the publisher). Calling the **Get** action will return the publisher in the response body.
```
return CreatedAtRoute("GetPublisher", new { id = publisherToAdd.Id
}, publisherToAdd);
```

10. Save all files and start the application (F5).
11. Open Postman and add the URL to the **Post** action in the **Publishers** controller.
    http://localhost:55098/api/publishers

12. Select **POST** in Postman's drop-down.
13. Click on the **Headers** link under the URL field. Add a header key named *Content-Type* with a value of *application/json*. This will ensure that the publisher object is sent as JSON to the action method.
14. Place a breakpoint on the first if-statement in the **Post** action in the **Publishers-Controller** class.
15. Click the **Send** button. Inspect the **publisher** parameter. It should be **null** since you didn't provide any publisher data.
16. Continue the execution and inspect the returned status code and body data. A *400 Bad Request* should have been returned to Postman.

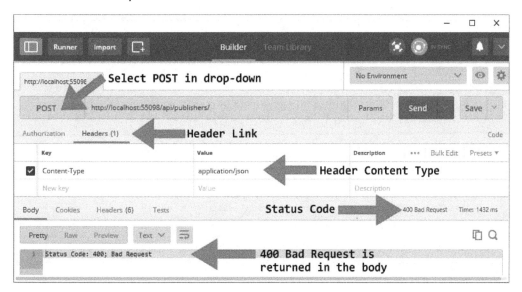

17. Click on the **Body** link to the right of the **Headers** link without making any changes to the previous post in Postman. Add the following publisher to the request body section. Note that the year is before the first recognized year in the if-statement you added earlier. You might have to select the **Raw** option to be able to add the data.

```
{
    "name": "Publishing House 3",
    "established": 1055
}
```

18. Click the **Send** button and inspect the **publisher** object in visual studio. It should contain the data you added to the request body.

19. Step through the code. The next if-statement should be triggered and a **ModelState** error should be added.

20. Continue stepping through the code until you hit the next if-statement where it should return *400 Bad Request* along with the error message. Press F5 to continue.

21. The error message should be displayed in the response body section in Postman (you might have to scroll down in Postman to see the response).

```
{ "Established": [
        "The oldest publishing house was founded in 1534." ] }
```

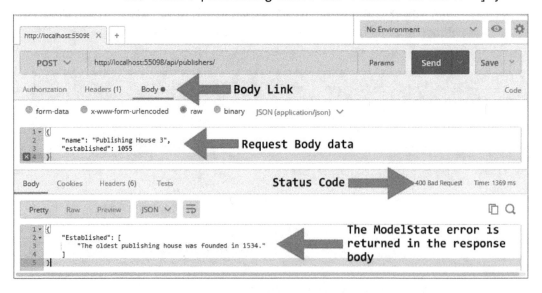

22. Remove the breakpoint in Visual Studio.

23. Change the *established* year to *2017* in the request data and click the **Send** button again.

```
{
    "name": "Publishing House 3",
    "established": 2017
}
```

24. The response data should display the added publisher (note the id value) because you called the **Get** action from the **Post** action with the **CreatedAtRoute** method. Also note the *201 Created* status code.

```
{
    "id": 3,
    "name": "Publishing House 3",
    "established": 2017,
    "bookCount": 0,
    "books": []
}
```

25. To verify that the publisher was added, you can call the **Get** action from Postman, sending in the id from the response body data. If you don't remember the URL, you can find it returned with the response data under the **Header** link. Don't forget to change the verb to **GET** in the drop-down before clicking the **Send** button.

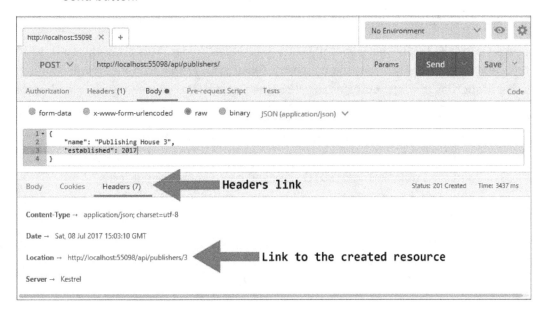

26. Close the browser when you have verified that the publisher was added. Note that the publisher will be removed when the browser is closed because you are working with in-memory data.

Update a Publisher (PUT)

You use the HTTP **Put** verb to update a whole resource—that is, all its properties. Contrast this with the HTTP **Patch** verb that let you update one or more properties in a partial update.

In this section, you will learn how to implement HTTP **Put** in a controller action and call it from Postman.

What's important to know with **Put** is that it will use default values for unassigned properties, such as **null** for strings and **0** for integers.

To be able to update a publisher in the data source, you need to add a method called **UpdatePublisher** to the service interface and the service class. The method should take a publisher id and a **PublisherUpdateDTO** object as parameters.

The **UpdatePublisher** method then updates the publisher object in the **Publishers** collection in the **MockData** class by calling the **GetPublisher** method to fetch the publisher matching the passed-in publisher id and assign new values to it.

Adding the PublisherUpdateDTO Class

Add a class called **PublisherUpdateDTO** to the *Models* folder. This class will be used to receive the request data from the consumer (Postman). In this scenario, it will have the same properties and attributes as the **PublisherCreateDTO**, so you can copy and paste them into the **PublisherUpdateDTO**.

1. Add a class called **PublisherUpdateDTO** to the *Models* folder.
2. Open the **PublisherCreateDTO** class and copy all properties and attributes.
3. Open the **PublisherUpdateDTO** class and paste in the copied code.
   ```
   [Required(ErrorMessage = "You must enter a name.")]
   [MaxLength(50)]
   public string Name { get; set; }
   public int Established { get; set; }
   ```

The complete code for the **PublisherUpdateDTO** class:

```
public class PublisherUpdateDTO
{
    [Required(ErrorMessage = "You must enter a name.")]
    [MaxLength(50)]
    public string Name { get; set; }
    public int Established { get; set; }
}
```

Adding the UpdatePublisher Method to the Service

1. Open the **IBookstoreRepository** interface.
2. Add a method definition for a method named **UpdatePublisher** that takes an **id** (**int**) and a **publisher** (**PublisherUpdateDTO**) instance as parameters and doesn't return anything.
   ```
   void UpdatePublisher(int id, PublisherUpdateDTO publisher);
   ```
3. Open the **BookstoreMockRepository** service class.
4. Add the **UpdatePublisher** method from the interface.
   ```
   public void UpdatePublisher(int id, PublisherUpdateDTO publisher)
   {
       throw new NotImplementedException();
   }
   ```
5. Remove the **throw** statement.
6. Fetch the publisher matching the **id** parameter by calling the **GetPublisher** method and store it in a variable named **publisherToUpdate**.
   ```
   var publisherToUpdate = GetPublisher(id);
   ```
7. Assign values from the **publisher** object passed-in to the method to the fetched publisher in the **publisherToUpdate** object.
   ```
   publisherToUpdate.Name = publisher.Name;
   publisherToUpdate.Established = publisher.Established;
   ```
8. Save all files.

The complete code for the **UpdatePublisher** method:

```
public void UpdatePublisher(int id, PublisherUpdateDTO publisher)
{
    var publisherToUpdate = GetPublisher(id);
    publisherToUpdate.Name = publisher.Name;
    publisherToUpdate.Established = publisher.Established;
}
```

The code in the **IBookstoreRepository** interface, so far:

```
public interface IBookstoreRepository
{
    IEnumerable<PublisherDTO> GetPublishers();
    PublisherDTO GetPublisher(int publisherId,
        bool includeBooks = false);
    void AddPublisher(PublisherDTO publisher);
    void UpdatePublisher(int id, PublisherUpdateDTO publisher);
    bool Save();
}
```

Adding the PublisherExists Method to the Service

Before adding a book to the data source, you need to check that the publisher exists. You can do this by counting the publishers with the passed-in id and return **true** if the number is 1.

The method should take one parameter, a publisher id, and return **true** if the publisher exists in the **Publishers** collection in the **MockData** class.

1. Open the **IBookstoreRepository** interface.
2. Add a method definition for a method named **PublisherExists** that takes one parameter called **publisherId** (**int**) and returns a **bool** value
   ```
   bool PublisherExists(int publisherId);
   ```
3. Open the **BookstoreMockRepository** service class.
4. Add the **PublisherExists** method from the interface.
   ```
   public bool PublisherExists(int publisherId)
   {
        throw new NotImplementedException();
   }
   ```
5. Remove the **throw** statement and return whether the publisher exists.
   ```
   return MockData.Current.Publishers.Count(p =>
        p.Id.Equals(publisherId)).Equals(1);
   ```
6. Save the files.

The complete code for the **PublisherExists** method:

```
public bool PublisherExists(int publisherId)
{
    return MockData.Current.Publishers.Count(p =>
        p.Id.Equals(publisherId)).Equals(1);
}
```

The code in the **IBookstoreRepository** interface, so far:

```
public interface IBookstoreRepository
{
    IEnumerable<PublisherDTO> GetPublishers();
    PublisherDTO GetPublisher(int publisherId, bool includeBooks = false);
    void AddPublisher(PublisherDTO publisher);
    void UpdatePublisher(int id, PublisherUpdateDTO publisher);
    bool Save();
    bool PublisherExists(int publisherId);
}
```

Adding the Put Action to the PublishersController Class

Add an **[HttpPut]** attribute with an *{id}* parameter above the **Put** action method you add. The action should take two parameters: **id** (**int**) that matches the *{id}* parameter in the attribute, and **publisher** (**PublisherUpdateDTO**) that is decorated with the **[FromBody]** attribute.

```
[HttpPut("{id}")]
public IActionResult Put(int id, [FromBody]PublisherUpdateDTO publisher)
```

You might wonder why the id is sent in as a separate parameter as opposed to sending it with the request body and receiving it in the **publisher** object. If you recall the table in chapter 3, ids should be passed into the action with the URL to follow the Representational State Transfer (REST) standard for URLs. If you do decide to send in the ids with the **publisher** object as well, you should check that they are the same before taking any action.

After the necessary *400 Bad Request* checks have been made, the publisher is fetched from the **Publishers** collection in the **MockData** class by calling the **GetPublisher** method you added earlier.

Then the property values of that object are changed to the values passed-in through the request body.

Even though the **Save** method in the repository doesn't have to be called in this scenario, it will need to be called later when EF is implemented.

Lastly, you return a *204 No Content* response status code. The reason you don't return anything from the action is that the consumer already has all the information.

1. Open the **PublishersController** class.
2. Add an **[HttpPut]** attribute below the **Post** action and give it an *{id}* parameter.
   ```
   [HttpPut("{id}")]
   ```
3. Add a public action method named **Put** that takes two parameters: **id (int)** that matches the *{id}* parameter in the attribute, and **publisher (PublisherUpdate-DTO)** that is decorated with the **[FromBody]** attribute, denoting that it will get its values from the request body. The action should return **IActionResult**.
   ```
   public IActionResult Put(int id, [FromBody]PublisherUpdateDTO
   publisher)
   {
   }
   ```
4. Copy the *400 Bad Request* checks from the **Post** action and paste them into the **Put** action.
   ```
   if (publisher == null) return BadRequest();

   if (publisher.Established < 1534)
       ModelState.AddModelError("Established",
           "The oldest publishing house was founded in 1534.");

   if (!ModelState.IsValid) return BadRequest(ModelState);
   ```
5. Call the **PublisherExist** method in the service to verify that a publisher matching the id passed-in through the **id** parameter exists.
   ```
   var publisherExists = _rep.PublisherExists(id);
   ```
6. Return *404 Not Found* if a publisher with the passed-in id doesn't exist.
   ```
   if (!publisherExists) return NotFound();
   ```
7. Update the publisher by calling the **UpdatePublisher** method you just added to the service, and then call the **Save** method in the service. You do this now so that you don't forget to do it later when working with EF; the same controller will be used for that scenario.
   ```
   _rep.UpdatePublisher(id, publisher);
   _rep.Save();
   ```

8. Return *204 No Content*.
   ```
   return NoContent();
   ```

9. Run the application and open Postman.

10. Send a **GET** request to fetch the first publisher and inspect the data.
    http://localhost:55098/api/publishers/1
    ```
    {
        "id": 1,
        "name": "Publishing House 1",
        "established": 1921,
        "bookCount": 0,
        "books": []
    }
    ```

11. Update the same resource by changing one or both of the **name** and **established** properties.
    a. Select **PUT** in the drop-down.
    b. Click the **Headers** link in the request section and verify that the *Content-Type* key is set to *application/json*; if not, add it.
    c. Click the **Body** link to the right of the **Headers** link.
    d. Change one or both values in the **Body** section.
    ```
    {
        "name": "Publishing House 11",
        "established": 2018
    }
    ```
    e. Click the **Send** button. A *204 No Content* status code should be returned if all goes well.
    f. Select **GET** in the drop-down and click the **Send** button.
    g. The altered publisher should be returned in the request body section along with a *200 OK* status code.
    ```
    {
        "id": 1,
        "name": "Publishing House 11",
        "established": 2018,
        "bookCount": 0,
        "books": []
    }
    ```
    h. Close the browser to stop the application. Remember that the changes aren't permanent since you are working with in-memory data.

The complete code for the **Put** action method:

```
[HttpPut("{id}")]
public IActionResult Put(int id, [FromBody]PublisherUpdateDTO publisher)
{
    if (publisher == null) return BadRequest();

    if (publisher.Established < 1534)
        ModelState.AddModelError("Established",
            "The oldest publishing house was founded in 1534.");

    if (!ModelState.IsValid) return BadRequest(ModelState);

    var publisherExists = _rep.PublisherExists(id);
    if (!publisherExists) return NotFound();

    _rep.UpdatePublisher(id, publisher);
    _rep.Save();

    return NoContent();
}
```

Partially Update a Publisher (PATCH)

Patch is similar to **Put**, with the difference that it performs a partial update. Instead of having to send all the property values, you can choose which properties to update.

The **Patch** request body is different from the **Put** request body. In this example where you are updating the value of the **Established** property, three key-value pairs must be used: *op*, which specifies the operation to perform (*replace*); *path*, which is the property to change; and *value*, which is the new value to store in the property.

```
[
    {
        "op": "replace",
        "path":"/established",
        "value": "1756"
    }
]
```

Another difference between **Patch** and **Put** is that **Patch** receives the **PublisherUpdate-DTO** object from the request body transformed into a **JsonPatchDocument**, which is used to merge the data with the data in the publisher you want to change in the data source.

```
[FromBody]JsonPatchDocument<PublisherUpdateDTO> publisher
```

1. Open the **PublishersController** class.
2. Add an **[HttpPatch]** attribute below the **Put** action and give it an *{id}* parameter.
   ```
   [HttpPatch("{id}")]
   ```
3. Add a **using** statement to the **JsonPatch** namespace to get access to the **Json-PatchDocument** type.
   ```
   using Microsoft.AspNetCore.JsonPatch;
   ```
4. Add a public action method named **Patch** that takes two parameters: **id** (**int**) that matches the *{id}* parameter in the attribute, and **publisher** (**JsonPatchDocument<PublisherUpdateDTO>**) that is decorated with the **[FromBody]** attribute, denoting that it will get its values from the request body. The action should return **IActionResult**.
   ```
   public IActionResult Patch(int id,
   [FromBody]JsonPatchDocument<PublisherUpdateDTO> publisher)
   {
   }
   ```
5. Return *400 Bad Request* if the passed-in publisher object is **null**.
   ```
   if (publisher == null) return BadRequest();
   ```
6. Fetch the publisher matching the passed-in id value. Return *404 Not Found* if the fetched publisher object is **null**.
   ```
   var publisherToUpdate = _rep.GetPublisher(id);
   if (publisherToUpdate == null) return NotFound();
   ```
7. Create a new instance of the **PublisherUpdateDTO** class and assign values to its properties from the fetched publisher. This object will be patched with values from the passed-in publisher object.
   ```
   var publisherPatch = new PublisherUpdateDTO()
   {
       Name = publisherToUpdate.Name,
       Established = publisherToUpdate.Established
   };
   ```

8. Patch the **publisherPatch** object you just created by calling the **ApplyTo** method on the passed-in **JsonPatchDocument publisher** instance. Pass in the **ModelState** object to the method to log any errors that occur.
```
publisher.ApplyTo(publisherPatch, ModelState);
```

9. Return *400 Bad Request* if a **ModelState** error has occurred in the patch process.
```
if (!ModelState.IsValid) return BadRequest(ModelState);
```

10. Copy the custom **Established** property check from the **Put** action and paste it into the **Patch** action. Change **publisher** to **publisherPatch**.
```
if (publisherPatch.Established < 1534)
    ModelState.AddModelError("Established",
        "The oldest publishing house was founded in 1534.");

if (!ModelState.IsValid) return BadRequest(ModelState);
```

11. Call the **UpdatePublisher** method and the **Save** method in the service and return a *204 No Content* from the **Patch** action.
```
_rep.UpdatePublisher(id, publisherPatch);
_rep.Save();
return NoContent();
```

12. Run the application and open Postman.

13. Send a **GET** request to fetch the first publisher and inspect the data.
http://localhost:55098/api/publishers/1
```
{
    "id": 1,
    "name": "Publishing House 1",
    "established": 1921,
    "bookCount": 0,
    "books": []
}
```

14. Update the **Established** property for the same resource.
   a. Select **PATCH** in the drop-down.
   b. Click the **Headers** link in the request section and verify that the *Content-Type* key is set to *application/json*; if not, add it.
   c. Click the **Body** link to the right of the **Headers** link.
   d. Add a JSON patch object that modifies the value in the *established* property in the **Body** section.

```
[
    {
        "op": "replace",
        "path":"/established",
        "value": "1756"
    }
]
```

e. Click the **Send** button. A *204 No Content* status code should be returned if all goes well.

f. Select **GET** in the drop-down and click the **Send** button.

g. The altered publisher should be returned in the response body section along with a *200 OK* status code.

```
{
    "id": 1,
    "name": "Publishing House 1",
    "established": 1756,
    "bookCount": 0,
    "books": []
}
```

h. Close the browser to stop the application. Remember that the changes aren't permanent since you are working with in-memory data.

The complete code for the **Patch** action method:

```
[HttpPatch("{id}")]
public IActionResult Patch(int id,
[FromBody]JsonPatchDocument<PublisherUpdateDTO> publisher)
{
    if (publisher == null) return BadRequest();

    var publisherToUpdate = _rep.GetPublisher(id);

    if (publisherToUpdate == null) return NotFound();

    var publisherPatch = new PublisherUpdateDTO()
    {
        Name = publisherToUpdate.Name,
        Established = publisherToUpdate.Established
    };

    publisher.ApplyTo(publisherPatch, ModelState);
```

```
    if (!ModelState.IsValid) return BadRequest(ModelState);

    if (publisherPatch.Established < 1534)
        ModelState.AddModelError("Established",
            "The oldest publishing house was founded in 1534.");

    if (!ModelState.IsValid) return BadRequest(ModelState);

    _rep.UpdatePublisher(id, publisherPatch);
    _rep.Save();

    return NoContent();
}
```

Delete a Publisher (DELETE)

Now that you have learned how to fetch, add, and update a resource, it is time to look at how you can delete a resource.

This requires you to define a new method in the **IBookstoreRepository** interface and then implement it in the **BookstoreMockRepository** service. The **DeletePublisher** method should take an instance of the **PublisherDTO** class as a parameter and not return anything (**void**).

Since the books related to a publisher should be removed with the publisher, you could add and implement a method called **DeleteBook** that takes an instance of the **BookDTO** class as a parameter and doesn't return anything. This method can then be reused when implementing the **Delete** action in the **BooksController** class.

When the books related to the publisher have been removed, the publisher itself should be removed.

Adding the DeleteBook Method to the Service

This method should remove one book from the **Books** collection in the **MockData** store.

1. Open the **IBookstoreRepository** interface.
2. Add a definition for a method called **DeleteBook** that takes an instance of the **BookDTO** class as a parameter and doesn't return anything.
   ```
   void DeleteBook(BookDTO book);
   ```

3. Open the **BookstoreMockRepository** service and implement the **DeleteBook** method.

```
    public void DeleteBook(BookDTO book)
    {
        throw new NotImplementedException();
    }
```

4. Remove the **throw** statement.
5. Remove the book from the **Books** collection in the **MockData** class.
   `MockData.Current.Books.Remove(book);`

6. Save all files.

The complete code for the **DeleteBook** method:

```
public void DeleteBook(BookDTO book)
{
    MockData.Current.Books.Remove(book);
}
```

Adding the DeletePublisher Method to the Service

This method should remove a publisher from the **Publishers** collection and its related books from the **Books** collection in the **MockData** store.

1. Open the **IBookstoreRepository** interface.
2. Add a definition for a method called **DeletePublisher** that takes an instance of the **PublisherDTO** class as a parameter and doesn't return anything.
   `void DeletePublisher(PublisherDTO publisher);`

3. Open the **BookstoreMockRepository** service and implement the **DeletePublisher** method.
   ```
   public void DeletePublisher(PublisherDTO publisher) {
       throw new NotImplementedException();
   }
   ```

4. Remove the **throw** statement.
5. Remove the books related to the publisher from the **Books** collection in the **MockData** class.
   ```
   foreach (var book in publisher.Books)
       DeleteBook(book);
   ```

6. Remove the publisher from the **Publishers** collection.
   `MockData.Current.Publishers.Remove(publisher);`

7. Save all files.

The complete code for the **DeletePublisher** method:

```
public void DeletePublisher(PublisherDTO publisher)
{
    foreach (var book in publisher.Books)
        DeleteBook(book);

    // Alternative implementation to remove the books from a publisher
    // MockData.Current.Books.RemoveAll(b =>
    //     b.PublisherId.Equals(publisher.Id));

    MockData.Current.Publishers.Remove(publisher);
}
```

The code for the **IBookstoreRepository** interface, so far:

```
public interface IBookstoreRepository
{
    IEnumerable<PublisherDTO> GetPublishers();
    PublisherDTO GetPublisher(int publisherId,
        bool includeBooks = false);
    void AddPublisher(PublisherDTO publisher);
    void DeletePublisher(PublisherDTO publisher);

    bool Save();

    void DeleteBook(BookDTO book);
}
```

Adding the Delete Action Method in the PublishersController Class

The last action you will implement in the **PublishersController** class is the **Delete** action. It takes an *{id}* parameter in the URI and a matching parameter called **id** in the method definition. The return data type should be **IActionResult**.

Begin by trying to fetch the publisher with the already implemented **GetPublisher** service method. Retrun a *404 Not Found* status code if the publisher doesn't exist.

If it does exist, then remove it from the **Publishers** collection in the **MockData** class by calling the **DeletePublisher** method you just added. Don't forget to call the **Save** method from the action.

Return a *204 No Content* status when the publisher has been successfully removed.

1. Open the **PublishersController** class.
2. Add an **[HttpDelete]** attribute that has an *{id}* parameter defined below the **Patch** action method.
   ```
   [HttpDelete("{id}")]
   ```
3. Add an action method named **Delete** that takes a parameter called **id (int)** and return **IActionResult**.
   ```
   public IActionResult Delete(int id)
   {
   }
   ```
4. Try to fetch the publisher matching the passed-in id and store the result in a variable called **publisherToDelete**.
   ```
   var publisherToDelete = _rep.GetPublisher(id);
   ```
5. Return *404 Not Found* if the publisher doesn't exist.
   ```
   if (publisherToDelete == null) return NotFound();
   ```
6. Delete the publisher by calling the **DeletePublisher** method in the service. Then call the **Save** method.
   ```
   _rep.DeletePublisher(publisherToDelete);
   _rep.Save();
   ```
7. Return *204 No Content* when the publisher has been successfully removed.
   ```
   return NoContent();
   ```
8. Start the application (F5) and open Postman.
9. Select **GET** in Postman's drop-down.
10. Enter the URL to fetch a list of all publishers and click the **Send** button. A result like the one shown below should be returned.
    http://localhost:55098/api/publishers

    ```
    [
        {
            "id": 1,
            "name": "Publishing House 1",
            "established": 1921,
            "bookCount": 0,
            "books": []
        },
        {
            "id": 2,
            "name": "Publishing House 2",
    ```

```
            "established": 1888,
            "bookCount": 0,
            "books": []
        }
    ]
```

11. Select **DELETE** in the drop-down and modify the URL to target one of the publishers by id.
    http://localhost:55098/api/publishers/1

12. Click the **Send** button. The response body should be empty since the action only returned a status code. If the publisher was successfully removed, the *204 No Content* status code should be displayed.

13. Select **GET** in the drop-down and modify the URL to fetch all publishers and click the **Send** button. The removed publisher should no longer be available.
    http://localhost:55098/api/publishers

```
    [
        {
            "id": 2,
            "name": "Publishing House 2",
            "established": 1888,
            "bookCount": 0,
            "books": []
        }
    ]
```

14. Close the browser to stop the application.

The complete code for the **Delete** action:

```
[HttpDelete("{id}")]
public IActionResult Delete(int id)
{
    var publisherToDelete = _rep.GetPublisher(id);
    if (publisherToDelete == null) return NotFound();

    _rep.DeletePublisher(publisherToDelete);
    _rep.Save();

    return NoContent();
}
```

Summary

In this chapter, you have implemented the **PublishersController** class to fetch and manipulate publishers in the in-memory **MockData** class.

By adding the method definitions to the **IBookstoreRepository** interface, you have made it possible to reuse those definitions later when adding Entity Framework to the mix.

You added and called methods in the **BookstoreMockRepository** service that modifies and fetches data in the in-memory **MockData** store.

You have also learned how to return correct status codes from Web API actions and how to call actions using Postman.

In the next chapter, you will implement the **BooksController** class, which enables the consuming application to fetch, add, update, and delete books in the **Books** collection in the in-memory **MockData** class.

8. Adding the Books Controller

Introduction

In this chapter, you will implement a second controller, for books. A book can only belong to one publisher, and since a book is tightly related to a publisher, you will use the same base route (*api/publishers*) used for publishers to fetch and manipulate books.

The route for books will always contain a publisher id, and a book id where applicable. A **POST** for instance never have a book id, only a publisher id, because the book hasn't been created yet and therefore doesn't have an id.

Route for **GET** (list) and **POST**: `api/publishers/{publisherId}/books`

Route for targeting a single book: `api/publishers/{publisherId}/books/{bookId}`

HTTP Verb	Attribute	Sample URI	
GET	HttpGet	api/publisher/1/books	(list)
		api/publisher/1/books/2	(book with id 2)
POST	HttpPost	api/publisher/1/books	
PUT	HttpPut	api/publisher/1/books/2	
PATCH	HttpPatch	api/publisher/1/books/2	
DELETE	HttpDelete	api/publisher/1/books/2	

```
[Route("api/publishers")]
public class BooksController : Controller
{
    [HttpGet("{publisherId}/books")]
    public IActionResult Get(int publisherId) { ... }

    [HttpPut("{publisherId}/books/{id}")]
    public IActionResult Put(int publisherId, int id,
    [FromBody]BookUpdateDTO book) { ... }
}
```

Adding the BooksController Class

Too keep the code clean and decluttered, it's good practice to use separate controllers for different purposes even if they are related, like publishers and books.

In this section, you will add the **BooksController** that will fetch and manipulate books related to a publisher. It will have the same base route (*api/publishers*) as the **Publishers-Controller** class.

To get access to the in-memory data, you will use dependency injection to inject an instance of the **BookstoreMockRepository** service using the **IBookstoreRepository** interface as the injected type. Store the service instance in a class-level variable to make it accessible throughout the controller.

1. Add a class called **BooksController** to the *Controllers* folder.
2. Inherit the **Controller** class to get access to basic controller functionality. You must resolve or add a **using** statement to the **Microsoft.AspNetCore.Mvc** namespace.
   ```
   public class BooksController : Controller
   {
   }
   ```
3. Add attribute routing to *api/publishers* above the class.
   ```
   [Route("api/publishers")]
   ```
4. Add a constructor to the class and the **IBookstoreRepository** interface as the dependency-injected type. When the controller is created an instance of the **BookstoreMockRepository** service will be injected through the interface. You need to add a **using** statement to the **Services** namespace.
   ```
   public BooksController(IBookstoreRepository rep)
   {
   }
   ```
5. Add a class-level variable to hold the injected instance.
   ```
   IBookstoreRepository _rep;
   ```
6. Assign the injected instance to the class-level variable inside the constructor.
   ```
   _rep = rep;
   ```
7. Save the controller.

The **BooksController** class, so far:

```
[Route("api/publishers")]
public class BooksController : Controller
{
    IBookstoreRepository _rep;

    public BooksController(IBookstoreRepository rep)
    {
        _rep = rep;
    }
}
```

Get a List of Books (GET)

To fetch a collection of books, you need the publisher id to narrow down the returned books to those related to a specific publisher. This action method is very similar to the **Get** action in the **PublishersController** class.

You need to add a method definition for a method called **GetBooks** to the **IBookstore-Repository**. The method should have a parameter called **publisherId** (**int**) and return **IEnumerable<BookDTO>**.

When you implement the method in the service class, use LINQ to fetch the books asscociated with the publisher matching the passed-in publisher id. The books are in the **Books** collection in the **MockData** class.

Use the **GetBooks** method in the **Get** action that you add to the **BooksController**.

Adding the GetBooks Method to the IBookstoreRepository Interface

1. Open the **IBookstoreRepository** Interface.
2. Add the method definition for the **GetBooks** method. It should have a parameter named **publisherId** (**int**) and return **IEnumerable<BookDTO>**.
   ```
   IEnumerable<BookDTO> GetBooks(int publisherId);
   ```
3. Add the **GetBooks** method to the **BookstoreMockRepository** service class.
   ```
   public IEnumerable<BookDTO> GetBooks(int publisherId)
   {
       throw new NotImplementedException();
   }
   ```
4. Remove the **throw** statement.

5. Return the books matching the passed-in publisher id from the **Books** collection in the **MockData** class.

```
return MockData.Current.Books.Where(b =>
    b.PublisherId.Equals(publisherId));
```

6. Save all files.

The code in the **IBookstoreRepository** interface, so far:

```
public interface IBookstoreRepository
{
    IEnumerable<PublisherDTO> GetPublishers();
    PublisherDTO GetPublisher(int publisherId, bool includeBooks = false);
    void AddPublisher(PublisherDTO publisher);
    void DeletePublisher(PublisherDTO publisher);
    bool Save();

    void DeleteBook(BookDTO book);
    IEnumerable<BookDTO> GetBooks(int publisherId);
}
```

The complete code for the **GetBooks** method in the **BookstoreMockRepository** class:

```
public IEnumerable<BookDTO> GetBooks(int publisherId)
{
    return MockData.Current.Books.Where(b =>
        b.PublisherId.Equals(publisherId));
}
```

Adding the Get Action Method to the BooksController Class

1. Open the **BooksController** Class.
2. Add an **[HttpGet]** attribute below the constructor. Since you need a publisher id to fetch the correct books, you need to add a *{publisherId}/books* URI to the attribute.

```
[HttpGet("{publisherId}/books")]
```

3. Add an action method named **Get** that takes a parameter called **publisherId (int)** and return **IActionResult**.

```
public IActionResult Get(int publisherId)
{
}
```

4. Fetch the books matching the passed-in publisher id by calling the **GetBooks** method you just added to the service class through the repository injected into the controller. Store the books in a variable called **books**.
```
var books = _rep.GetBooks(publisherId);
```

5. Return the books along with a *200 OK* status code.
```
return Ok(books);
```

6. Save all files.
7. Run the application (F5) and open Postman.
8. Select **GET** in Postman's drop-down.
9. Enter a URL to a publisher's books.
http://localhost:55098/api/publishers/1/books

10. Click the **Send** button. The response should look something like this:
```
[
    {
        "id": 2,
        "title": "Book 2",
        "publisherId": 1
    },
    {
        "id": 4,
        "title": "Book 4",
        "publisherId": 1
    }
]
```

11. Close the browser to stop the application.

The complete code in the **Get** action:

```
[HttpGet("{publisherId}/books")]
public IActionResult Get(int publisherId)
{
    var books = _rep.GetBooks(publisherId);

    return Ok(books);
}
```

Get a Book (GET)

To fetch a single book, you need the publisher id and the book id. This action method is very similar to the previous **Get** action, but it takes two parameters: **publisherId** and **id** (the book id) to find a single book related to a specific publisher.

You need to add a method definition for a method called **GetBook** to the **IBookstore-Repository**. The method should have two parameters, called **publisherId (int)** and **Id (int)**, and return an instance of the **BookDTO** class.

When you implement the method in the service class, use LINQ to fetch the book matching the passed-in publisher id and book id. The books are in the **Books** collection in the **Mock-Data** class

Call the **GetBook** method from the **Get** action that you will add to the **BooksController**. The **Get** action should be reachable by the name **GetBook** from other actions. You name the action by adding the **Name** property to the **[HttpGet]** attribute. Later, you will call this action from the **Post** action.

```
[HttpGet("{publisherId}/books/{id}", Name = "GetBook")]
```

Adding the GetBook Method to the IBookstoreRepository Interface

1. Open the **IBookstoreRepository** Interface.
2. Add the method definition for the **GetBook** method. It should take two parameters: **publisherId (int)** and **Id (int)**, and return an instance of the **BookDTO** class.
   ```
   BookDTO GetBook(int publisherId, int bookId);
   ```
3. Add the **GetBook** method to the **BookstoreMockRepository** service class.
   ```
   public BookDTO GetBook(int publisherId, int bookId) {
       throw new NotImplementedException();
   }
   ```
4. Remove the **throw** statement.
5. Return the book matching the passed-in publisher id and book id from the **Books** collection in the **MockData** class.
   ```
   return MockData.Current.Books.FirstOrDefault(b =>
           b.PublisherId.Equals(publisherId) &&
           b.Id.Equals(bookId));
   ```
6. Save all files.

The complete code for the **GetBook** method in the **BookstoreMockRepository** class:

```
public BookDTO GetBook(int publisherId, int bookId)
{
    return MockData.Current.Books.FirstOrDefault(b =>
        b.PublisherId.Equals(publisherId) &&
        b.Id.Equals(bookId));
}
```

Adding the Get Action Method to the BooksController Class

1. Open the **BooksController** Class.
2. Add an **[HttpGet]** attribute below the previous action. Since you need a publisher id and a book id to fetch the correct books, you need to add a *{publisherId}/books/{id}* URI to the attribute. Because this action will be called from the **Post** action, it needs a unique name (*GetBook*) specified with the **Name** property of the **[HttpGet]** attribute.
    ```
    [HttpGet("{publisherId}/books/{id}", Name = "GetBook")]
    ```

3. Add an action method named **Get** that takes two parameters: **publisherId** (**int**) and **id** (**int**) and return **IActionResult**.
    ```
    public IActionResult Get(int publisherId, int id)
    {
    }
    ```

4. Fetch the book matching the passed-in publisher id and book id by calling the **GetBook** method you just added to the service class using the repository injected into the controller. Store the books in a variable called **book**.
    ```
    var book = _rep.GetBook(publisherId, id);
    ```

5. Return a *404 Not Found* status code if the book wasn't found.
    ```
    if (book == null) return NotFound();
    ```

6. Return the books along with a *200 OK* status code.
    ```
    return Ok(books);
    ```

7. Save all files.
8. Run the application (F5) and open Postman.
9. Select **GET** in Postman's drop-down.
10. Enter a URL to a publisher's book.
    http://localhost:55098/api/publishers/1/books/4

11. Click the **Send** button. The response should look something like this:

```
{
    "id": 4,
    "title": "Book 4",
    "publisherId": 1
}
```

12. Now let's try to fetch a book that doesn't exist. Change the book id to a non-existing id in the URL and click the **Send** button again. The status code in Postman should show *404 Not Found*.
    http://localhost:55098/api/publishers/1/books/40

13. Now let's change the URL to a publisher that doesn't exist and send the request again. The status code in Postman should show *404 Not Found*.
    http://localhost:55098/api/publishers/100/books/4

14. Close the browser to stop the application.

The complete code in the **Get** action:

```
[HttpGet("{publisherId}/books/{id}", Name = "GetBook")]
public IActionResult Get(int publisherId, int id)
{
    var book = _rep.GetBook(publisherId, id);

    if (book == null) return NotFound();

    return Ok(book);
}
```

Add a Book (POST)

The **Post** method will receive its data from the request body. To collect that data in the action method, you use the **[FromBody]** attribute on the parameter receiving the data. ASP.NET will then automatically match the properties in the incoming data with properties in the parameter object. To follow the URI standard you have used so far, the action method must receive a parameter called **publisherId (int)**.

```
[HttpPost("{publisherId}/books")]
public IActionResult Post(int publisherId, [FromBody]BookCreateDTO book)
```

When receiving data for an update, the object created for the parameter won't have an id since it doesn't exist in the data source yet. It is therefore common to use a separate DTO class to represent the *create* object. You will add a new class to the *Models* folder for a

DTO class called **BookCreateDTO**. The class will have two properties: **Title** (**string**) and **PublisherId** (**int**).

To help the client determine how to use the properties and report errors for certain scenarios, you use data annotation attributes on properties where needed. Let's say for instance that the **Title** property is a required field that can hold a maximum of 50 characters. To enforce this behavior you could add the **[Required]** and **[MaxLength]** attributes to it. To gain access to the data annotation attributes, you have to add a **using** statement to the **System.ComponentModel.DataAnnotations** namespace.

There are certain checks that you need to do in the **Post** action to ensure that the correct data and status code are returned from the action.

- Check if the DTO is **null**, and if so, return *400 Bad Request*.
- Check if the publisher exists, and return *404 Not Found* if it doesn't exist.
- Check the **ModelState** object to see if any model state errors exist and return a bad request and the model state if there are errors.

If the validation succeeds, you create a new instance of the **BookDTO** and assign property values from the **BookCreateDTO** instance. You then add the **BookDTO** to the data source.

To be able to add the book to the data source, you need to add a method called **AddBook** to the service interface and the service class. The method should take the newly created **BookDTO** object as its only parameter.

The **AddBook** method then adds the book object to the **Books** collection in the **MockData** class by calling the **Add** method on the collection.

When the book has been saved, you redirect to the **GetBook** route (the latest **Get** action you added) by calling the **CreateAtRoute** method with the route name, the **Get** action parameters, and the added book object. If you recall, you added a name to the **Get** action that returns a single book using the **[HttpGet]** attribute for this reason.

Adding the BookCreateDTO Class
Since the book doesn't exist in the data source yet, it hasn't got an id. It would therefore be pointless to have an **Id** property in the DTO class. To separate the different scenarios for adding and updating resources from fetching data, it is common practice to use separate DTOs for these three scenarios. The DTOs for updating and adding resources will have the same properties in this project, but in a real-world scenario, they might not.

1. Add a class called **BookCreateDTO** to the *Models* folder.
2. Add two properties to the class: **Title (string)** and **PublisherId (int)**.
3. Add two data annotations to the **Title** property: **MaxLength(50)** and **Required**, with its *ErrorMessage* property set to *You must enter a title*.
   ```
   [Required(ErrorMessage = "You must enter a title.")]
   [MaxLength(50)]
   ```
4. Save the class.

The complete code for the **BookCreateDTO** class:

```
public class BookCreateDTO
{
    [Required(ErrorMessage = "You must enter a title")]
    [MaxLength(50)]
    public string Title { get; set; }
    public int PublisherId { get; set; }
}
```

Adding the AddBook Method to the Service

1. Open the **IBookstoreRepository** interface.
2. Add a method definition for a method named **AddBook** that takes a **BookDTO** instance as a parameter and doesn't return anything.
   ```
   void AddBook(BookDTO book);
   ```
3. Open the **BookstoreMockRepository** service class.
4. Add the **AddBook** method from the interface.
   ```
   public void AddBook(BookDTO book) {
       throw new NotImplementedException();
   }
   ```
5. Remove the **throw** statement.
6. Because the collections in the **MockData** class can't generate ids automatically, like a database, you must manually create a new id for the publisher. You can do this by calling the **Max** LINQ method on the collection and increment the value by 1. Assign the new id to the passed-in book object. Note that you do this for demo purposes only.
   ```
   var bookId = MockData.Current.Books.Max(m => m.Id) + 1;
   book.Id = bookId;
   ```
7. Add the book object to the **Books** collection.
   ```
   MockData.Current.Books.Add(book);
   ```

8. Save all files.

The complete code for the **AddBook** method:

```
public void AddBook(BookDTO book)
{
    // For Demo purposes only: Get next id
    var bookId = MockData.Current.Books.Max(m => m.Id) + 1;
    book.Id = bookId;

    MockData.Current.Books.Add(book);
}
```

The code for the **IBookstoreRepository** interface, so far:

```
public interface IBookstoreRepository
{
    IEnumerable<PublisherDTO> GetPublishers();
    PublisherDTO GetPublisher(int publisherId,
        bool includeBooks = false);
    void AddPublisher(PublisherDTO publisher);
    void DeletePublisher(PublisherDTO publisher);
    bool Save();
    bool PublisherExists(int publisherId);

    void DeleteBook(BookDTO book);
    IEnumerable<BookDTO> GetBooks(int publisherId);
    BookDTO GetBook(int publisherId, int bookId);
    void AddBook(BookDTO book);
}
```

Adding the Post Action to the BooksController Class

1. Open the **BooksController** class.
2. Add an **[HttpPost]** attribute with a *publisherId* parameter below the previously added **Get** methods.
   ```
   [HttpPost("{publisherId}/books")]
   ```
3. Add a public method called **Post** that returns **IActionResult** and takes two parameters: **publisherId (int)** and **book (BookCreateDTO)** that is decorated with the **[FromBody]** attribute. You need to add a **using** statement to the **Models** namespace to gain access to the class. The attribute ensures that the object is assigned from data in the request body sent from the client, which in this case will be Postman.

```
[HttpPost("{publisherId}/books")]
public IActionResult Post(int publisherId, [FromBody]BookCreateDTO
book)
{
}
```

4. The first check you must add to the action is to see if the passed-in object is **null**, and if so, return *400 Bad Request*.
```
if (book == null) return BadRequest();
```

5. Return *400 Bad Request* and the **ModelState** object if the model state is invalid.
```
if (!ModelState.IsValid) return BadRequest(ModelState);
```

6. Check that the publisher exists by calling the **PublisherExists** method you added to the service earlier. Return a *404 Not Found* status code if the publisher doesn't exist.
```
var publisherExists = _rep.PublisherExists(publisherId);
if (!publisherExists) return NotFound();
```

7. Create an instance of the **BookDTO** class called **bookToAdd** and assign the values from the **book** and **publisherId** parameters. You shouldn't assign a value to the **Id** property because it will be assigned automatically in the **AddBook** method.
```
var bookToAdd = new BookDTO { PublisherId = publisherId,
    Title = book.Title };
```

8. Add the book object stored in the **bookToAdd** variable to the **Books** collection in the **MockData** class by calling the **AddBook** method you just added to the repository service. Call the **Save** method; even though it isn't necessary for this scenario, it will enable you to switch to an Entity Framework service later without modifying the controller.
```
_rep.AddBook(bookToAdd);
_rep.Save();
```

9. The last bit of code you need to add is a call to the **GetBook** action with the **CreatedAtRoute** method; this will call an existing **Get** action reusing its code. The first parameter is the name of the action to call, the second is an anonymous object containing values for the **Get** action's parameters, and the last parameter is the added source object (the book).
```
return CreatedAtRoute("GetBook", new {
    publisherId = publisherId, id = bookToAdd.Id }, bookToAdd);
```

10. Save all files and start the application (F5).
11. Open Postman and enter the URL to the **Post** action in the **BooksController** class.

http://localhost:55098/api/publishers/1/books

12. Select **POST** in Postman's drop-down.
13. Click on the **Headers** link under the URL field. Add a header key named *Content-Type* with a value of *application/json*. This will ensure that the book object is sent as JSON to the action method.
14. Place a breakpoint on the first if-statement in the **Post** action in the **Books-Controller** class.
15. Click the **Send** button in Postman. Inspect the **book** parameter; it should be **null** since you didn't provide any book data.
16. Remove the breakpoint from the **Post** action.
17. Continue the execution (F5) and inspect the returned status code and body data. A *400 Bad Request* should have been returned to Postman.
18. Click on the **Body** link to the right of the **Headers** link without making any changes to the previous post in Postman. Add the following book to the request body section. You might have to select the **Raw** option to be able to add the data. The publisher id is assigned from the URI's *publisherId* parameter.

```
{
    "title": "New Book"
}
```

19. Click the **Send** button to send the request to add the book.
20. The response data should display the added book (note the id value) because you called the **Get** action from the **Post** action with the **CreatedAtRoute** method. Also note the *201 Created* status code.

```
{
    "id": 5,
    "title": "New Book",
    "publisherId": 1
}
```

21. To make sure that the book was added, you can call the **Get** action from Postman, sending in the id from the response body data. If you don't remember the URL, you can find it returned with the response data under the **Header** link in the **Response** section. Don't forget to change the verb to **GET** in the drop-down.
22. Close the browser when you have verified that the book was added. Note that the book will be removed when the browser is closed because you are working with in-memory data.

The complete code for the **Post** action in the **BooksController** class:

```
[HttpPost("{publisherId}/books")]
public IActionResult Post(int publisherId, [FromBody]BookCreateDTO book)
{
    if (book == null) return BadRequest();
    if (!ModelState.IsValid) return BadRequest(ModelState);

    var publisherExists = _rep.PublisherExists(publisherId);
    if (!publisherExists) return NotFound();

    var bookToAdd = new BookDTO { PublisherId = publisherId,
        Title = book.Title };

    _rep.AddBook(bookToAdd);
    _rep.Save();

    return CreatedAtRoute("GetBook", new { publisherId = publisherId,
        id = bookToAdd.Id }, bookToAdd);
}
```

Update a Book (PUT)

In this section, you will implement the HTTP **Put** action in the **BooksController** class and call it from Postman.

What's important to know with **Put** is that it will use default values for unassigned properties, such as **null** for strings and **0** for integers.

Adding the BookUpdateDTO Class

Add a class called **BookUpdateDTO** to the *Models* folder. This class will be used to receive the request data from the consumer (Postman). In this scenario, it will have the same properties and attributes as the **BookCreateDTO**, so you can copy and paste them into the **BookUpdateDTO**.

1. Add a class called **BookUpdateDTO** to the *Models* folder.
2. Open the **BookCreateDTO** class and copy all properties and attributes.
3. Open the **BookUpdateDTO** class and paste in the copied code. Change *name* to *title* in the *ErrorMessage* property.
   ```
   [Required(ErrorMessage = "You must enter a title")]
   [MaxLength(50)]
   public string Title { get; set; }
   ```

```
    public int PublisherId { get; set; }
```

The complete code for the **BookUpdateDTO** class:

```
public class BookUpdateDTO
{
    [Required(ErrorMessage = "You must enter a title")]
    [MaxLength(50)]
    public string Title { get; set; }
    public int PublisherId { get; set; }
}
```

Adding the UpdateBook Method to the Service

1. Open the **IBookstoreRepository** interface.
2. Add a method definition for a method named **UpdateBook** that takes a
   publisherId (int), a **bookId (int)**, and a **book (BookUpdateDTO)** instance as
   parameters and doesn't return anything.
   ```
   void UpdateBook(int publisherId, int bookId, BookUpdateDTO book);
   ```

3. Open the **BookstoreMockRepository** service class.
4. Add the **UpdateBook** method from the interface.
   ```
   public void UpdateBook(int publisherId, int bookId, BookUpdateDTO
   book) {
       throw new NotImplementedException();
   }
   ```

5. Remove the **throw** statement.
6. Fetch the book matching the **publisherId** and **bookId** parameters by calling the
   GetBook method.
   ```
   var bookToUpdate = GetBook(publisherId, bookId);
   ```

7. Assign values from the **book** object passed-in to the method to the fetched book
   in the **bookToUpdate** object.
   ```
   bookToUpdate.Title = book.Title;
   ```

8. Save all files.

The complete code for the **UpdateBook** method:

```
public void UpdateBook(int publisherId, int bookId, BookUpdateDTO book)
{
    var bookToUpdate = GetBook(publisherId, bookId);
    bookToUpdate.Title = book.Title;
}
```

The code in the **IBookstoreRepository** interface, so far:

```
public interface IBookstoreRepository
{
    IEnumerable<PublisherDTO> GetPublishers();
    PublisherDTO GetPublisher(int publisherId,
        bool includeBooks = false);
    void AddPublisher(PublisherDTO publisher);
    void DeletePublisher(PublisherDTO publisher);
    bool Save();
    bool PublisherExists(int publisherId);

    void DeleteBook(BookDTO book);
    IEnumerable<BookDTO> GetBooks(int publisherId);
    BookDTO GetBook(int publisherId, int bookId);
    void AddBook(BookDTO book);
    void UpdateBook(int publisherId, int bookId, BookUpdateDTO book);
}
```

Adding the Put Action to the BooksController Class

Add an **[HttpPut]** attribute with two parameters: *{publisherId}* and *{id}* above the **Put** action you add. The action method should take three parameters: **publisherId** (**int**) and **id** (**int**) that matches the *{publisherId}* and *{id}* attribute parameters, and **book** (**BookUpdate-DTO**) that is decorated with the **[FromBody]** attribute.

```
[HttpPut("{publisherId}/books/{id}")]
public IActionResult Put(int publisherId, int id,
[FromBody]BookUpdateDTO book)
```

You might wonder why the ids are sent in as separate parameters as opposed to sending them with the request body and receive it in the **book** object. If you recall the table from the beginning of this chapter, ids should be passed into the action with the URL to follow the REST standard. If you do decide to send in the ids with the **book** object as well, you should check that they are the same as the ones in the URL before taking any action.

After the necessary *400 Bad Request* checks have been made, the book is fetched from the **Books** collection in the **MockData** class by calling the **GetBook** method you added earlier.

Then the property values of that object are changed to the values passed-in through the request body by calling the **UpdateBook** method in the service.

Even though the **Save** method in the repository doesn't have to be called in this scenario, it must be called later when EF is implemented, so you might as well add it now.

Lastly, you return a *204 No Content* response status. The reason you don't return anything from the action is that the consumer already has all the information.

1. Open the **BooksController** class.
2. Add an **[HttpPut]** attribute with two parameters: *{publisherId}* and *{id}* below the **Post** action.
   ```
   [HttpPut("{publisherId}/books/{id}")]
   ```
3. Add a public action method named **Put** that takes three parameters: **publisherId** (**int**) and **id** (**int**), and **book** (**BookUpdateDTO**) that is decorated with the **[FromBody]** attribute, denoting that it will get its values from the request body. The action should return **IActionResult**.
   ```
   public IActionResult Put(int publisherId, int id,
   [FromBody]BookUpdateDTO book)
   {
   }
   ```
4. Copy the *400 Bad Request* checks from the **Post** action and paste them into the **Put** action.
   ```
   if (book == null) return BadRequest();
   if (!ModelState.IsValid) return BadRequest(ModelState);
   ```
5. Call the **GetBook** method in the service to fetch the book matching the publisher id and book id passed-in through the **publisherId** and **id** parameters.
   ```
   var bookToUpdate = _rep.GetBook(publisherId, id);
   ```
6. Return *404 Not Found* if a publisher or a book with the passed-in ids doesn't exist.
   ```
   if (bookToUpdate == null) return NotFound();
   ```
7. Assign property values from the request body to the fetched book and call the **Save** method in the service. You do this now so that you don't forget to do it later when working with EF; the same controller will be used for that scenario.
   ```
   _rep.UpdateBook(publisherId, id, book);
   _rep.Save();
   ```
8. Return *204 No Content*.
   ```
   return NoContent();
   ```
9. Run the application and open Postman.

10. Send a **Get** request to fetch a book related to the first publisher and inspect the data.

    http://localhost:55098/api/publishers/1/books/2

    ```
    {
        "id": 2,
        "title": "Book 2",
        "publisherId": 1
    }
    ```

11. Update the same resource by changing the **title** property.
    a. Select **PUT** in the drop-down.
    b. Click the **Headers** link in the request section and verify that the *Content-Type* key is set to *application/json*; if not, add it.
    c. Click the **Body** link to the right of the **Headers** link.
    d. Change the title in the **Body** section.
    ```
    {
        "title": "Altered Title"
    }
    ```
    e. Click the **Send** button. A *204 No Content* status code should be returned if all goes well.
    f. Select **GET** in the drop-down and click the **Send** button.
    g. The altered book should be returned in the request body section along with a *200 OK* status code.
    ```
    {
        "id": 2,
        "title": "Altered Title",
        "publisherId": 1
    }
    ```
    h. Close the browser to stop the application. Remember that the changes aren't permanent since you are working with in-memory data.

The complete code for the **Put** action method:

```
[HttpPut("{publisherId}/books/{id}")]
public IActionResult Put(int publisherId, int id,
[FromBody]BookUpdateDTO book)
{
    if (book == null) return BadRequest();
    if (!ModelState.IsValid) return BadRequest(ModelState);
```

```
var bookToUpdate = _rep.GetBook(publisherId, id);
if (bookToUpdate == null) return NotFound();

_rep.UpdateBook(publisherId, id, book);
_rep.Save();

return NoContent();
}
```

Partial Update of a Book (PATCH)

Patch is similar to **Put**, with the difference being it performs a partial update. Instead of having to send all the property values, you can choose which properties to update.

The **Patch** request body is different from the **Put** request body. In this example where you are updating the value of the **Title** property, three key-value pairs must be used: *op*, which specifies the operation to perform (*replace*); *path*, which is the property to change; and *value*, which is the new value to store in the property.

```
[
    {
        "op": "replace",
        "path":"/title",
        "value": "The patched title"
    }
]
```

Another difference between **Patch** and **Put** is that **Patch** receives the **BookUpdateDTO** object from the request body transformed into a **JsonPatchDocument**.

[FromBody]JsonPatchDocument<BookUpdateDTO> book

1. Open the **BooksController** class.
2. Add a **using** statement to the **JsonPatch** namespace to get access to the **Json-PatchDocument** type.
   using Microsoft.AspNetCore.JsonPatch;
3. Copy the whole **Put** action and its attribute and paste it in below the code you copied.
4. Rename the attribute **[HttpPatch]**.
   [HttpPatch("{publisherId}/books/{id}")]

5. Rename the action method **Patch** and change the **BookUpdateDTO** type to **JsonPatchDocument<BookUpdateDTO>**.

```
public IActionResult Patch(int publisherId, int id,
[FromBody]JsonPatchDocument<BookUpdateDTO> book)
{
}
```

6. Create a new instance of the **BookUpdateDTO** class between the last if-statement and the property assignments and assign values to its properties from the fetched book. This object will be patched with values from the passed-in **book** object.

```
var bookToPatch = new BookUpdateDTO()
{
    PublisherId = bookToUpdate.PublisherId,
    Title = bookToUpdate.Title
};
```

7. Use the JSON patch to merge the passed-in book with the **bookToPatch** object you just created by calling the **ApplyTo** method on the passed-in **JsonPatchDocument book** instance. Pass in the **ModelState** object to the method to log any errors that occur.

```
book.ApplyTo(bookToPatch, ModelState);
```

8. Return *400 Bad Request* if a **ModelState** error has occurred in the patch process.

```
if (!ModelState.IsValid) return BadRequest(ModelState);
```

9. Run the application (F5) and open Postman.

10. Send a **GET** request to fetch one of the books for the first publisher and inspect the data.

   http://localhost:55098/api/publishers/1/books/2

```
{
    "id": 2,
    "title": "Book 2",
    "publisherId": 1
}
```

11. Update the **Title** property for the same resource.
    a. Select **PATCH** in the drop-down.
    b. Click the **Headers** link in the request section and verify that the *Content-Type* key is set to *application/json*; if not, add it.
    c. Click the **Body** link to the right of the **Headers** link.

d. Change one or both values in the **Body** section.

```
[
    {
        "op": "replace",
        "path":"/title",
        "value": "The patched title"
    }
]
```

e. Click the **Send** button. A *204 No Content* status code should be returned if all goes well.

f. Select **GET** in the drop-down and click the **Send** button.

g. The altered book should be returned in the response body section along with a *200 OK* status code.

```
{
    "id": 2,
    "title": "The patched title",
    "publisherId": 1
}
```

h. Close the browser to stop the application. Remember that the changes aren't permanent since you are working with in-memory data.

The complete code for the **Patch** action method:

```
[HttpPatch("{publisherId}/books/{id}")]
public IActionResult Patch(int publisherId, int id,
[FromBody]JsonPatchDocument<BookUpdateDTO> book)
{
    if (book == null) return BadRequest();
    if (!ModelState.IsValid) return BadRequest(ModelState);

    var bookToUpdate = _rep.GetBook(publisherId, id);
    if (bookToUpdate == null) return NotFound();

    var bookToPatch =
        new BookUpdateDTO()
        {
            PublisherId = bookToUpdate.PublisherId,
            Title = bookToUpdate.Title
        };

    book.ApplyTo(bookToPatch, ModelState);
```

```
    if (!ModelState.IsValid) return BadRequest(ModelState);

    _rep.UpdateBook(publisherId, id, bookToPatch);
    _rep.Save();

    return NoContent();
}
```

Delete a Book (DELETE)

To delete a book, you call the **DeleteBook** method in the service from the **Delete** action in the controller. Since you already have implemented the **DeleteBook** method in the previous chapter, you simply need to call it.

The first thing you do in the action method is to fetch the book matching the **publisherId** and **id** (book id) passed-in to the method; you do this by calling the **GetBook** method in the service.

Return a *404 Not Found* status code if the book wasn't found.

Call the **DeleteBook** method to remove the book and the **Save** method to persist the changes (not strictly necessary for this scenario, but it is needed in the EF scenario that you will implement in the next part of the book).

Return a *204 No Content* status code to show that the resource was successfully removed.

The complete code for the **DeleteBook** method you added in a previous chapter:

```
public void DeleteBook(BookDTO book)
{
    MockData.Current.Books.Remove(book);
}
```

1. Open the **BooksController** class.
2. Add an **HttpDelete** attribute with a book URI. The URI should have two parameters: *publisherId* and *Id*.
   ```
   [HttpDelete("{publisherId}/books/{id}")]
   ```
3. Add an action method that returns **IActionResult** and takes two parameters: **publisherId** and **Id**.
   ```
   public IActionResult Delete(int publisherId, int id)
   { ... }
   ```

4. Fetch the book matching the passed-in ids and store it in a variable called **book**.
   ```
   var book = _rep.GetBook(publisherId, id);
   ```

5. Check if the book exists and return a *404 Not Found* status code if the book isn't found.
   ```
   if (book == null) return NotFound();
   ```

6. Remove the book by calling the **DeleteBook** method in the service and persist the changes by calling the **Save** method.
   ```
   _rep.DeleteBook(book);
   _rep.Save();
   ```

7. Return a *204 No Content* status code to show that the resource was successfully removed.
   ```
   return NoContent();
   ```

8. Save all files.

9. Run the application and open Postman.

10. Send a **GET** request to fetch one of the books for the first publisher and inspect the data.
    http://localhost:55098/api/publishers/1/books/2
    ```
    {
        "id": 2,
        "title": "Book 2",
        "publisherId": 1
    }
    ```

11. Change to **DELETE** in the drop-down and click the **Send** button to remove the book. A *204 No Content* status code should be returned and the response body should be empty.

12. Change back to **GET** in the drop-down and click the **Send** button to try to fetch the book again. A *404 Not Found* status code should be returned.

13. To be really certain that the book has been removed, you can select **GET** in the drop-down and click the **Send** button after changing the URL to get all books for the same publisher. The book you removed should not be in the response body.
    http://localhost:55098/api/publishers/1/books

14. Close the browser to stop the application.

The complete code for the **Delete** Action in the **BooksController** class:

```
[HttpDelete("{publisherId}/books/{id}")]
public IActionResult Delete(int publisherId, int id)
{
    var book = _rep.GetBook(publisherId, id);

    if (book == null) return NotFound();

    _rep.DeleteBook(book);
    _rep.Save();

    return NoContent();
}
```

Summary

In this chapter, you have implemented the **BooksController** class to fetch and manipulate books in the in-memory **MockData** store.

By adding the method definitions to the **IBookstoreRepository** interface, you have made it possible to reuse those definitions later when adding Entity Framework to the mix.

You added and called methods in the **BookstoreMockRepository** service that modifies data in the in-memory **MockData** source.

You have also learned how to return correct status codes from Web API actions and how to call actions using Postman.

This is the last chapter in this part of the book.

In the next part, you will implement a new data service that uses Entity Framework to fetch and update data in a database. Then you will switch from in-memory data to a database by instantiating the database service instead of the **BookstoreMockRepository** in the **Startup** class.

Part 3:
Creating an Entity
Framework Service

9. Entity Classes

Introduction

In this chapter, you will add the entity classes needed to store data in the database. Since you already have added DTO classes, you can use them for reference when adding the **Publisher** and **Book** entity classes. Each entity class will represent a table in the database you will create in the next chapter.

The two DTO classes that most closely match the entities you will create are the **PublisherDTO** and the **BookDTO**.

The code in the **PublisherDTO** class:

```
public class PublisherDTO
{
    public int Id { get; set; }
    public string Name { get; set; }
    public int Established { get; set; }

    public int BookCount { get { return Books.Count; } }

    public ICollection<BookDTO> Books { get; set; } =
        new List<BookDTO>();
}
```

The code in the **BookDTO** class:

```
public class BookDTO
{
    public int Id { get; set; }
    public string Title { get; set; }
    public int PublisherId { get; set; }
}
```

Adding the Publisher and Book Entity Classes

Looking at the **BookDTO** class, you can see that it has the same properties needed in the **Book** entity, with one exception: The entity class should reference the **Publisher** entity since there is a one-to-many relationship between the tables.

Looking at the **PublisherDTO** class, you can see that the **BookCount** property is a calculated property that shouldn't be stored in the database. Also note that the **Books** collection property references the **BookDTO** class; this must be changed to the **Book** entity class since the **Publishers** table should reference the **Books** table in a one-to-many relationship.

To make the **Id** property in the **Publisher** and **Book** entity classes an auto generated primary key in the respective tables, you need to add the **[Key]** and **[DatabaseGenerated]** attributes to both **Id** properties.

You also want the **Title** and **Name** properties to be required fields in the tables; to accomplish this you add the **[Required]** attribute to them. Let's restrict the number of characters to 50 for both fields in the database by adding the **[MaxLength(50)]** attribute.

Although you don't need to specify that the foreign key in the **Book** table is the **PublisherId** property, you can do so by adding the **[ForeignKey]** attribute to it. By convention EF will look at the referenced table and use a property named **Id** or the table name prefixed with *Id*. If the property used for the foreign key isn't named as the convention dictates, the **[ForeignKey]** attribute tells EF which property to use as the foreign key.

1. Add a folder named *Entities* to the project.
2. Add a class named **Book** to the *Entities* folder.
3. Add a class named **Publisher** to the *Entities* folder.
4. Open the **PublisherDTO** class and copy all properties.
5. Open the **Publisher** class and paste in the copied properties.
6. Remove the **BookCount** property. It's a calculated property that shouldn't be in the database, and since each property will become a column in the table, it shouldn't be present.
7. Change **BookDTO** to **Book** for the **Books** collection property. The collection property tells EF that the **Book** entity will fulfill the many-part in the one-to-many relationship between the two tables.
   ```
   public ICollection<Book> Books { get; set; } = new List<Book>();
   ```
8. Add **using** statements to the **DataAnnotations** and **DataAnnotations.Schema** namespaces to gain access to the attributes you will add.
   ```
   using System.ComponentModel.DataAnnotations;
   using System.ComponentModel.DataAnnotations.Schema;
   ```

9. Add the **[Key]** and **[DatabaseGenerated]** attributes to the **Id** property.
```
[Key]
[DatabaseGenerated(DatabaseGeneratedOption.Identity)]
public int Id { get; set; }
```

10. Add the **[Required]** and **[MaxLength(50)]** attributes to the **Name** property.
```
[Required]
[MaxLength(50)]
public string Name { get; set; }
```

11. Open the **BookDTO** class and copy all the properties.

12. Open the **Book** class and paste in the copied properties.

13. Add **using** statements to the **DataAnnotations** and **DataAnnotations.Schema** namespaces to gain access to the attributes you will add.
```
using System.ComponentModel.DataAnnotations;
using System.ComponentModel.DataAnnotations.Schema;
```

14. Add the **[Key]** and **[DatabaseGenerated]** attributes to the **Id** property.
```
[Key]
[DatabaseGenerated(DatabaseGeneratedOption.Identity)]
public int Id { get; set; }
```

15. Add the **[Required]** and **[MaxLength(50)]** attributes to the **Title** property.
```
[Required]
[MaxLength(50)]
public string Title { get; set; }
```

16. Add the **[ForeignKey]** attribute to the **PublisherId** property, specifying that it should be used as the foreign key from the **Publisher** table.
```
[ForeignKey("PublisherId")]
public int PublisherId { get; set; }
```

17. Add the **Publisher** class to specify that a relation exists between the two tables. The **Publisher** entity will fulfill the one-part in the one-to-many relationship between the two tables.
```
public Publisher Publisher { get; set; }
```

18. Save all files.

The complete code for the **Publisher** entity class:

```
public class Publisher
{
    [Key]
    [DatabaseGenerated(DatabaseGeneratedOption.Identity)]
    public int Id { get; set; }
    [Required]
    [MaxLength(50)]
    public string Name { get; set; }
    public int Established { get; set; }

    public ICollection<Book> Books { get; set; } = new List<Book>();
}
```

The complete code for the **Book** entity class:

```
public class Book
{
    [Key]
    [DatabaseGenerated(DatabaseGeneratedOption.Identity)]
    public int Id { get; set; }
    [Required]
    [MaxLength(50)]
    public string Title { get; set; }

    [ForeignKey("PublisherId")]
    public int PublisherId { get; set; }
    public Publisher Publisher { get; set; }
}
```

Summary

In this chapter, you added the **Publisher** and **Book** entity classes and their properties and attributes.

In the next chapter, you will install Entity Framework Core and transform each entity class into a table in the database you will create.

10. Entity Framework and AutoMapper

Introduction

In this chapter, you will set up Entity Framework (EF) and get familiar with how it works. To work with EF, you must install the proper services, either manually in the *.csproj* file or by using the NuGet manager.

When the services have been installed and configured in the **Startup** class, you need to add a data context class that inherits from the **DbContext** class. This class will be the context that you use to interact with the database. To add a table to the database, the table's entity class must be added as a **DbSet** property in the context class.

When the services are installed and configured in the **Startup** class, you create the first migration by using the Package Manager Console and the **Add-Migration** command. When the initial migration has been added, the database can be generated with the **Update-Database** command.

If you make any changes to the database, like adding or changing columns or tables, then you must execute the **Add-Migration** and **Update-Database** commands again for the application to work properly.

Installing Entity Framework and User Secrets

Now you will install the Entity Framework NuGet packages needed to create and interact with a database. The database you add later will use the built-in local development SQL Server version, which installs with Visual Studio 2017. You will also use User Secrets, stored in a file named *secrets.json*, to store the database connection string securely.

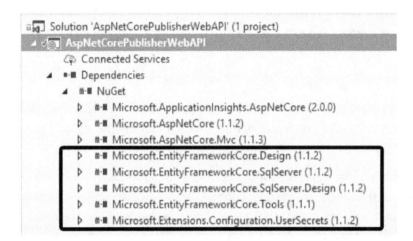

1. Open the NuGet Manager. Right click on the project node and select **Manage NuGet Packages**, or add them manually to the *.csproj* file.

2. Install the following four packages: **Microsoft.EntityFrameworkCore.Design**, **Microsoft.EntityFrameworkCore.SqlServer**, **Microsoft.EntityFrameworkCore.SqlServer.Design**, **Microsoft.EntityFrameworkCore.Tools**.

3. Open the *.csproj* file and verify that the packages have been installed.
   ```
   <PackageReference
       Include="Microsoft.EntityFrameworkCore.Design"
       Version="1.1.2" />
   <PackageReference
       Include="Microsoft.EntityFrameworkCore.SqlServer"
       Version="1.1.2" />
   <PackageReference
       Include="Microsoft.EntityFrameworkCore.SqlServer.Design"
       Version="1.1.2" />
   <PackageReference
       Include="Microsoft.EntityFrameworkCore.Tools"
       Version="1.1.1" />
   ```

4. Check that the *User Secrets* NuGet packages have been installed with stable versions to be able to store and retrieve data in the *secrets.json* file.
   ```
   <PackageReference
       Include="Microsoft.Extensions.Configuration.UserSecrets"
       Version="1.1.2" />
   <DotNetCliToolReference
       Include="Microsoft.Extensions.SecretManager.Tools"
       Version="1.0.1" />
   ```

Adding the SqlDbContext Class

Now that the NuGet packages have been installed, you can add a class called **SqlDbContext** that inherits form the **DbContext** class. This class will be your connection to the database. It defines the entity classes as **DbSet** properties, which are mirrored as tables in the database.

For the **AddDbContext** method to be able to add the context to the services collection in the **Startup** class, the **SqlDbContext** must have a constructor with a **DbContextOptions< SqlDbContext>** parameter, which passes the parameter object to its base constructor.

1. Add a class called **SqlDbContext** to the *Entities* folder in the Solution Explorer.
2. Let the **SqlDbContext** class inherit the **DbContext** class. The **DbContext** class is in the **Microsoft.EntityFrameworkCore** namespace.
   ```
   public class SqlDbContext : DbContext
   {
   }
   ```
3. Add **DbSet** properties for the **Publisher** and **Book** classes in the **SqlDbContext** class.
   ```
   public DbSet<Publisher> Publishers { get; set; }
   public DbSet<Book> Books { get; set; }
   ```
4. Add the constructor with the a **DbContextOptions<SqlDbContext>** parameter.
   ```
   public SqlDbContext(DbContextOptions<SqlDbContext> options)
   : base(options)
   {
   }
   ```
5. Save all the files.

The complete code for the **SqlDbContext** class:

```
public class SqlDbContext : DbContext
{
    public DbSet<Publisher> Publishers { get; set; }
    public DbSet<Book> Books { get; set; }

    public SqlDbContext(DbContextOptions<SqlDbContext> options)
    : base(options)
    {
    }
}
```

Configuration in the Startup Class

Before the initial migration can be applied, you must configure Entity Framework to use the **SqlDbContext**, and read the connection string from the *secrets.json* file. Using the *secrets.json* file has two purposes: It stores the connection string in a safe place that is not checked into source control. It also renders the *appsettings.json* obsolete for storing secret or sensitive data locally, which is a good thing, since it is checked into source control.

If the *appsettings.json* file isn't optional, the migration might fail.

1. Right click on the project node in the Solution Explorer and select **Manage User Secrets**.
2. Add the following connection string property. Note that the database name is **BookstoreDb**, and that the connection string must be written on a single line in the *secrets.json* file because it's a string.
    ```
    "connectionStrings": {
        "sqlConnection":
            "Data Source=(localdb)\\MSSQLLocalDB;
            Initial Catalog=BookstoreDb;Integrated Security=True;"
    }
    ```
3. Open the **Startup** class and locate the constructor.
4. Add the **optional: true** parameter value to the **AddJsonFile** method for the *appsettings.json* file.
    ```
    .AddJsonFile("appsettings.json", optional: true);
    ```
5. Locate the **ConfigureServices** method and fetch the connection string from the *secrets.json* file using the **Configuration** object. Store the connection string in a variable called **conn**.
    ```
    var conn = Configuration["connectionStrings:sqlConnection"];
    ```
6. Use the **AddDbContext** method on the **services** collection to add the database context and the EF services at the beginning of the **ConfigureServices** method. Call the **UseSqlServer** method on the **options** action in its constructor to specify that you want to use a SQL Server database provider. The **UseSqlServer** method is in the **Microsoft.EntityFrameworkCore** namespace. Pass in the **conn** variable to the **UseSqlServer** method.
    ```
    services.AddDbContext<SqlDbContext>(options =>
        options.UseSqlServer(conn));
    ```

The complete code for the *secrets.json* file:

```
{
    "Message": "Hello, from secrets.json",

    "connectionStrings": {
        "sqlConnection":
            "Data Source=(localdb)\\MSSQLLocalDB;
            Initial Catalog=BookstoreDb;Integrated Security=True;"
    }
}
```

*Note that the **sqlConnection** property value should be one line of code.*

The complete code for the **Startup** class's constructor:

```
public Startup(IHostingEnvironment env)
{
    var builder = new ConfigurationBuilder()
        .SetBasePath(Directory.GetCurrentDirectory())
        .AddJsonFile("appsettings.json", optional:true);

    if (env.IsDevelopment())
        builder.AddUserSecrets<Startup>();

    Configuration = builder.Build();
}
```

The complete code for the **Startup** class's **ConfigureServices** method:

```
public void ConfigureServices(IServiceCollection services)
{
    services.AddMvc();

    var conn = Configuration["connectionStrings:sqlConnection"];
    services.AddDbContext<SqlDbContext>(options =>
        options.UseSqlServer(conn));

    services.AddScoped(typeof(IBookstoreRepository),
        typeof(BookstoreMockRepository));
}
```

Adding the Initial Migration and Creating the Database

To add the initial migration and create the database, you execute the **Add-Migration** and **Update-Database** commands in the Package Manager Console (**View-Other Windows-Package Manager Console**).

When the **Add-Migration** command has been successfully executed, a new folder called *Migrations* will appear in the project. The current and all future migrations will be stored in this folder.

If you encounter the error message *No parameterless constructor was found on 'SqlDbContext': Either add a parameterless constructor to 'SqlDbContext' or add an implementation of 'IDbContextFactory<SqlDbContext>' in the same assembly as 'SqlDbContext',* then check that your connection string in *secrets.json* is correct, that the **optional** parameter has been added to the to the **AddJsonFile** method and is assigned **true**, and that the connection string is loaded in the **Startup** class, before doing any other troubleshooting.

1. Open the Package Manager Console.
2. Type in the command *add-migration Initial* and press **Enter**. Note the *Migrations* folder that has been added and the migration files in it.
3. Execute the command *update-database* in the Package Manager Console to create the database.
4. Open the **SQL Server Object Explorer** from the **View** menu.
5. Expand the **MSSQLLocalDb** node, and then the **Databases** node. If the **BookstoreDb** database isn't visible, right click on the **Databases** node and select **Refresh**.
6. Expand the **BookstoreDb** node, and then the **Tables** node. You should now see the **Publishers** and **Books** tables in the **BookstoreDb** database that you just created.
7. Expand the **Publishers** table and then the **Columns** node. You should now see the columns in the table. Note that they match the properties in the **Publisher** entity class, and that they have the restrictions from the attributes you added to its properties. Now do the same for the **Books** table and **Book** entity class.

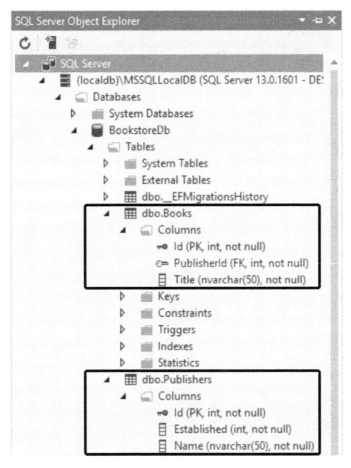

8. Right click on the **Publishers** table and select **View Data**. This will open the table in edit mode. Add the same publishers you added to the **MockData** class (see image below). Press **Enter** to commit the values on a row when adding the publishers. Do the same for the **Books** table.

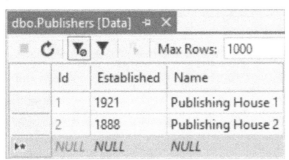

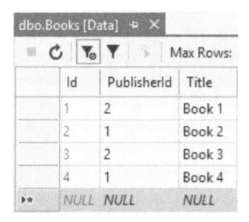

Installing AutoMapper

AutoMapper is an object-to-object mapper that will be used to map entity (database table) objects to Data Transfer Objects (DTOs), transforming one into the other.

Note that the property names don't have to be the same in the DTO and the entity. Auto-Mapper can be configured to map between properties with different names. It can also use auto-mapping between properties with identical names.

You can either add the following row to the <ItemGroup> node in the *.csproj* file manually and save the file, or use the NuGet manager to add AutoMapper.

```
<PackageReference Include="AutoMapper" Version="6.0.2" />
```

The following listing shows you how to use the NuGet manager to install packages.

1. Right click on the **Dependencies** node in the Solution Explorer and select **Manage NuGet Packages** in the context menu.

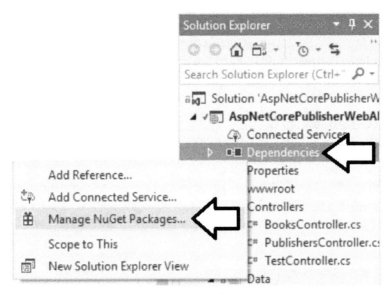

2. Click on the **Browse** link at the top of the dialog (see image below).
3. Select **nuget.org** in the drop-down to the far right in the dialog.
4. Type *AutoMapper* in the textbox.
5. Select the **AutoMapper** package in the list; it will probably be the first package in the list.
6. Make sure that you use the latest stable version (6.0.2).
7. Click the **Install** button.

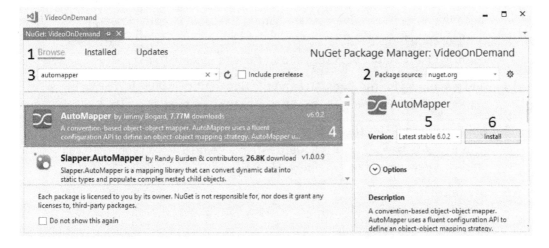

To verify that the package has been installed, you can open the *.csproj* file by right clicking on the project node and select **Edit AspNetCorePublisherWebAPI.csproj**, or you can expand the **Dependencies-NuGet** folder in the Solution Explorer. You might have to restart Visual Studio after saving the file.

Configuring AutoMapper

For AutoMapper to work properly, you must add configuration to the **ConfigureServices** method in the *Startup.cs* file. The configuration tells AutoMapper how to map between objects, in this case between entities and DTOs. Default mapping can be achieved by specifying the class names of the objects to be mapped, without naming specific properties. With default matching, only properties with the same name in both classes will be matched.

A more granular mapping can be made by specifying exactly which properties that match; this allows the property names to differ in the classes.

1. Open the *Startup.cs* file and locate the **ConfigureServices** method and go to the end of the method.

2. Call the action (**config**) in AutoMapper's **Initialize** method.
   ```
   AutoMapper.Mapper.Initialize(config =>
   {
   }
   ```

3. Add a mapping for the **Book** entity and **BookDTO** classes inside the **config** block. Since the properties of interest are named the same in both classes, no specific configuration is necessary.
   ```
   config.CreateMap<Entities.Book, Models.BookDTO>();
   ```

4. Add a mapping for the **BookDTO** and the **Book** entity inside the **config** block.
   ```
   config.CreateMap<Models.BookDTO, Entities.Book>();
   ```

5. Now do the same for the **Publisher** entity class and the **PublisherDTO**.
   ```
   config.CreateMap<Entities.Publisher, Models.PublisherDTO>();
   config.CreateMap<Models.PublisherDTO, Entities.Publisher>();
   ```

6. Save all files.

The complete AutoMapper configuration in the **ConfigurationServices** method:

```
AutoMapper.Mapper.Initialize(config =>
{
    config.CreateMap<Entities.Book, Models.BookDTO>();
    config.CreateMap<Models.BookDTO, Entities.Book>();
    config.CreateMap<Entities.Publisher, Models.PublisherDTO>();
    config.CreateMap<Models.PublisherDTO, Entities.Publisher>();
});
```

Adding the BookstoreSqlRepository Service Component

To use the database in the application, you implement the **IBookstoreRepository** interface in a new service component class called **BookstoreSqlRepository**. Then, you change the service registration in the **ConfigureServices** method in the **Startup** class to create instances of the new component.

Implementing the BookstoreSqlRepository Service Component Class

Let's begin by implementing the **BookstoreSqlRepository** class that will communicate with the database through the **SqlDbContext** you added in the previous chapter.

1. Add a class called **BookstoreSqlRepository** to the *Services* folder.
2. Open the **Startup** class and change the service registration for the **IBookstore-Repository** interface to create instances of the **BookstoreSqlRepository** class.
    ```
    services.AddScoped(typeof(IBookstoreRepository),
        typeof(BookstoreSqlRepository));
    ```
3. Add a private field called **_db** for the **SqlDbContext** class in the **BookstoreSqlRepository** class. This variable will hold the context needed to communicate with the database. You need to add a **using** statement to the **AspNetCorePublisherWebAPI.Entities** namespace to get access to the database context.
    ```
    private SqlDbContext _db;
    ```
4. Add a constructor and inject an instance of the **SqlDbContext** class; name the parameter **db**. Assign the injected object in the **db** parameter to the **_db** variable.
    ```
    public BookstoreSqlRepository(SqlDbContext db)
    {
        _db = db;
    }
    ```

5. Implement the **IBookstoreRepository** interface. You can use the lightbulb button when hovering over the interface name.
```
public class BookstoreSqlRepository : IBookstoreRepository
```

6. Add a **using** statement to the **AutoMapper** namespace to be able to map objects.
```
using AutoMapper;
```

7. Remove the **throw** statement in the **AddBook** method. Add a mapping between the **BookDTO** class and the **Book** entity class and store the object in a variable called **bookToAdd**. Call the **Add** method on the **Books** collection in the **_db** context and pass in the **bookToAdd** object to the method.
```
public void AddBook(BookDTO book)
{
    var bookToAdd = Mapper.Map<Book>(book);
    _db.Books.Add(bookToAdd);
}
```

8. Remove the **throw** statement in the **AddPublisher** method. Add a mapping between the **PublisherDTO** class and the **Publisher** entity class and store the object in a variable called **publisherToAdd**. Call the **Add** method on the **Publishers** collection in the **_db** context and pass in the **publisherToAdd** object to the method.
```
public void AddPublisher(PublisherDTO publisher)
{
    var publisherToAdd = Mapper.Map<Publisher>(publisher);
    _db.Publishers.Add(publisherToAdd);
}
```

9. Remove the **throw** statement in the **UpdateBook** method. Fetch the book to update from the **Books** collection in the **_db** context and store it in a variable called **bookToUpdate;** use the passed-in **BooksId** and **PublisherId** parameters. Check that the book exists before assigning values to the fetched book from the passed-in book.
```
public void UpdateBook(int publisherId, int bookId, BookUpdateDTO book) {
    var bookToUpdate = _db.Books.FirstOrDefault(b =>
        b.Id.Equals(bookId) && b.PublisherId.Equals(publisherId));

    if (bookToUpdate == null) return;

    bookToUpdate.Title = book.Title;
```

```
        bookToUpdate.PublisherId = book.PublisherId;
    }
```

10. Remove the **throw** statement in the **UpdatePublisher** method. Fetch the
    publisher to update from the **Publishers** collection in the **_db** context and store
    it in a variable called **publisherToUpdate;** use the passed-in **id** parameter. Check
    that the publisher exists before assigning values to the fetched book from the
    passed-in book.

```
public void UpdatePublisher(int id, PublisherUpdateDTO publisher)
{
    var publisherToUpdate = _db.Publishers.FirstOrDefault(p =>
        p.Id.Equals(id));

    if (publisherToUpdate == null) return;

    publisherToUpdate.Name = publisher.Name;
    publisherToUpdate.Established = publisher.Established;
}
```

11. Remove the **throw** statement in the **DeleteBook** method. Fetch the book to
    delete from the **Books** collection in the **_db** context and store the book in a
    variable called **bookToDelete**. Use the **Id** and **PublisherId** properties in the
    passed-in **BookDTO** object to fetch the book to delete. Call the **Remove** method
    on the **Books** collection in the **_db** context and pass in the **bookToDelete** object
    to the method if the book exists.

```
public void DeleteBook(BookDTO book)
{
    var bookToDelete = _db.Books.FirstOrDefault(b =>
        b.Id.Equals(book.Id) &&
        b.PublisherId.Equals(book.PublisherId));

    if (bookToDelete != null) _db.Books.Remove(bookToDelete);
}
```

12. Implement the **DeletePublisher** in the same way as the **DeleteBook** method, but
    use the **Publishers** collection and **publisher** parameter.

```
public void DeletePublisher(PublisherDTO publisher)
{
    var publisherToDelete = _db.Publishers.FirstOrDefault(p =>
        p.Id.Equals(publisher.Id));
    if (publisherToDelete != null)
        _db.Publishers.Remove(publisherToDelete);
}
```

13. Remove the **throw** statement in the **GetBook** method. Fetch the book from the **Books** collection in the **_db** context and store it in a variable called **book**. Use the **bookId** and **publisherId** method parameters to fetch the book from the database. Map the fetched **Book** entity object to a **BookDTO** object using AutoMapper. Store the mapped object in a variable called **bookDTO**. Return the **bookDTO** object.

```
public BookDTO GetBook(int publisherId, int bookId)
{
    var book = _db.Books.FirstOrDefault(b =>
        b.Id.Equals(bookId) && b.PublisherId.Equals(publisherId));

    var bookDTO = Mapper.Map<BookDTO>(book);
    return bookDTO;
}
```

14. Implement the **GetBooks** method in a similar way to the **GetBook** method. Note that the entities are mapped to **IEnumerable<BookDTO>** because a collection is returned.

```
public IEnumerable<BookDTO> GetBooks(int publisherId)
{
    var books = _db.Books.Where(b =>
        b.PublisherId.Equals(publisherId));

    var bookDTOs = Mapper.Map<IEnumerable<BookDTO>>(books);

    return bookDTOs;
}
```

15. Remove the **throw** statement in the **GetPublisher** method.
    a. Fetch the publisher from the **Publishers** collection in the **_db** context and store it in a variable called **publisher**.
    b. If the publisher exists and the **includeBooks** parameter is **true**, then load the books related to the publisher.
    c. Use AutoMapper to map the publisher entity to an instance of the **PublisherDTO** class and store the object in a variable called **publisherDTO**.
    d. Return the object in the **publisherDTO** variable.

```
public PublisherDTO GetPublisher(int publisherId, bool
includeBooks = false)
{
    var publisher = _db.Publishers.FirstOrDefault(p =>
        p.Id.Equals(publisherId));

    if (includeBooks && publisher != null)
    {
        _db.Entry(publisher).Collection(c => c.Books).Load();
    }

    var publisherDTO = Mapper.Map<PublisherDTO>(publisher);

    return publisherDTO;
}
```

16. Remove the **throw** statement in the **GetPublishers** method and return the mapped **PublisherDTO** collection.
```
public IEnumerable<PublisherDTO> GetPublishers()
{
    return Mapper.Map<IEnumerable<PublisherDTO>>(_db.Publishers);
}
```

17. Remove the **throw** statement in the **PublisherExists** method and return **true** if the number of publishers in the **Publishers** collection matching the passed-in id is equal to 1.
```
public bool PublisherExists(int publisherId)
{
    return _db.Publishers.Count(p =>
        p.Id.Equals(publisherId)) == 1;
}
```

18. Remove the **throw** statement in the **Save** method. Call the **SaveChanges** method on the **_db** context object to persist all changes tracked by Entity Framework. Return **true** if the number of persisted row changes is greater than or equal to 0.
```
public bool Save()
{
    return _db.SaveChanges() >= 0;
}
```

19. Save all files.

The complete code in the **BookstoreSqlRepository** class:

```
public class BookstoreSqlRepository  : IBookstoreRepository
{
    private SqlDbContext _db;
    public BookstoreSqlRepository(SqlDbContext db)
    {
        _db = db;
    }

    public void AddBook(BookDTO book)
    {
        var bookToAdd = Mapper.Map<Book>(book);
        _db.Books.Add(bookToAdd);
    }

    public void AddPublisher(PublisherDTO publisher)
    {
        var publisherToAdd = Mapper.Map<Publisher>(publisher);
        _db.Publishers.Add(publisherToAdd);
    }

    public void UpdateBook(int publisherId, int bookId,
    BookUpdateDTO book)
    {
        var bookToUpdate = _db.Books.FirstOrDefault(b =>
            b.Id.Equals(bookId) && b.PublisherId.Equals(publisherId));

        if (bookToUpdate == null) return;

        bookToUpdate.Title = book.Title;
        bookToUpdate.PublisherId = book.PublisherId;
    }

        public void DeleteBook(BookDTO book)
    {
        var bookToDelete = _db.Books.FirstOrDefault(b =>
            b.Id.Equals(book.Id) &&
            b.PublisherId.Equals(book.PublisherId));
        if (bookToDelete != null) _db.Books.Remove(bookToDelete);
    }
```

```
public void UpdatePublisher(int id, PublisherUpdateDTO publisher)
{
    var publisherToUpdate = _db.Publishers.FirstOrDefault(p =>
        p.Id.Equals(id));

    if (publisherToUpdate == null) return;

    publisherToUpdate.Name = publisher.Name;
    publisherToUpdate.Established = publisher.Established;
}

public void DeletePublisher(PublisherDTO publisher)
{
    var publisherToDelete = _db.Publishers.FirstOrDefault(p =>
        p.Id.Equals(publisher.Id));
    if (publisherToDelete != null)
        _db.Publishers.Remove(publisherToDelete);
}

public BookDTO GetBook(int publisherId, int bookId)
{
    var book = _db.Books.FirstOrDefault(b => b.Id.Equals(bookId)
        && b.PublisherId.Equals(publisherId));
    var bookDTO = Mapper.Map<BookDTO>(book);

    return bookDTO;
}

public PublisherDTO GetPublisher(int publisherId,
bool includeBooks = false)
{
    var publisher = _db.Publishers.FirstOrDefault(p =>
        p.Id.Equals(publisherId));

    if (includeBooks && publisher != null)
    {
        _db.Entry(publisher).Collection(c => c.Books).Load();
    }

    var publisherDTO = Mapper.Map<PublisherDTO>(publisher);

    return publisherDTO;
}
```

```
public IEnumerable<BookDTO> GetBooks(int publisherId)
{
    var books = _db.Books.Where(b =>
        b.PublisherId.Equals(publisherId));
    var bookDTOs = Mapper.Map<IEnumerable<BookDTO>>(books);

    return bookDTOs;
}

public IEnumerable<PublisherDTO> GetPublishers()
{
    return Mapper.Map<IEnumerable<PublisherDTO>>(_db.Publishers);
}

public bool PublisherExists(int publisherId)
{
    return _db.Publishers.Count(p => p.Id.Equals(publisherId)) == 1;
}

public bool Save()
{
    return _db.SaveChanges() >= 0;
}
```
}

Using the BookstoreSqlRepository Service Component

Now that the **BookstoreSqlRepository** Service has been implemented and configured in the **Startup** class, it is time to test the functionality with Postman.

Not that you don't have to make any changes to either the **PublishersController** or **BooksController** classes for the WebAPI to fetch and manipulate data in the database. The only thing you needed to do was to implement the **BookstoreSqlRepository** Service and change the service registration in the **ConfigureServices** method.

When you begin fetching, adding, updating and deleting the data, the database should have the following data (you can modify the data manually in the tables if needed).

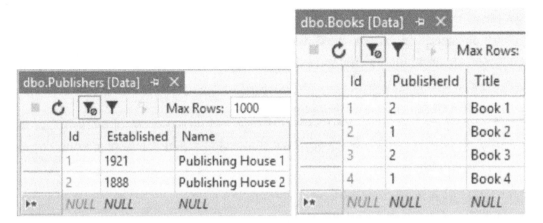

Start the application and open Postman.

Fetching All Publishers

To fetch all publishers, the **GetPublishers** method in the **BookstoreSqlRepository** service class is called through the **Get** action in the **PublishersController** class:

1. Enter the following URL: *http://localhost:55098/api/publishers*
2. Select **GET** in Postman's drop-down.
3. Click the **Send** button.
4. A *200 OK* response status code is returned along with an array of publishers from the **Publishers** table.

```
[
    {
        "id": 1,
        "name": "Publishing House 1",
        "established": 1921,
        "bookCount": 0,
        "books": []
    },
    {
        "id": 2,
        "name": "Publishing House 2",
        "established": 1888,
        "bookCount": 0,
        "books": []
    }
]
```

Fetching One Publisher

To fetch one specific publisher, the **GetPublisher** method in the **BookstoreSqlRepository** service class is called through the **Get** action in the **PublishersController** class:

1. Enter the following URL: *http://localhost:55098/api/publishers/1*
2. Select **GET** in Postman's drop-down.
3. Click the **Send** button.
4. A *200 OK* response status code is returned along with the desired publisher from the **Publishers** table.

```
{
    "id": 1,
    "name": "Publishing House 1",
    "established": 1921,
    "bookCount": 0,
    "books": []
}
```

Fetching a Publisher with Its Related Books

To fetch a specific publisher with its related books, the **GetPublisher** method in the **BookstoreSqlRepository** service class is called through the **Get** action in the **Publishers-Controller** class with the **includeBooks** parameter set to **true**:

1. URL: *http://localhost:55098/api/publishers/1?includeBooks=true*
2. Select **GET** in Postman's drop-down.
3. Click the **Send** button.
4. A *200 OK* response status code is returned along with the desired publisher from the **Publishers** table and its related books from the **Books** table.

```
{
    "id": 1,
    "name": "Publishing House 1",
    "established": 1921,
    "bookCount": 2,
    "books": [
        {
            "id": 2,
            "title": "Book 2",
            "publisherId": 1
        },
        {
```

```
            "id": 4,
            "title": "Book 4",
            "publisherId": 1
        }
    ]
}
```

Fetching a Non-Existing Publisher

You can do this with or without fetching the related books. Call the **GetPublisher** method in the **BookstoreSqlRepository** service class with a publisher id that doesn't exist with the **Get** action in the **PublishersController** class:

1. URL: *http://localhost:55098/api/publishers/1000*
2. Select **GET** in Postman's drop-down.
3. Click the **Send** button.
4. A *404 Not Found* response status code is returned because the **Publishers** table doesn't contain a publisher with id *1000*. The following code in the **Get** action triggered the error because the **GetPublisher** method that tried to fetch the publisher returned **null**.
    ```
    if (publisher == null) return NotFound();
    ```

Adding a Publisher

To add a publisher, the **AddPublisher** method in the **BookstoreSqlRepository** service class is called through the **Post** action in the **PublishersController** class:

1. Enter the following URL: *http://localhost:55098/api/publishers*
2. Select **POST** in Postman's drop-down.
3. Make sure that the *Content-Type* key is assigned *application/json* in the **Headers** section.
4. Enter the publisher's data in the request **Body** section.
    ```
    {
            "Name": "Publishing House 3",
            "Established": "2017"
    }
    ```
5. Click the **Send** button.
6. A *201 Created* response status code is returned along with the added publisher.

7. Open the **Publishers** table in the database and verify that the publisher was added. You can click the **Refresh** button above the table data if the table already is open.

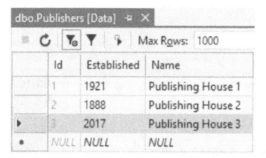

8. Fetch all publishers like you did in the *Fetching All Publishers* section and verify that the new publisher is returned in the array.

9. Now remove the body data and click the **Send** button again to try to add a publisher without data. This should trigger the code below and return a *400 Bad Request* status code. Check the **Publishers** table to verify that no publisher was added.
```
if (publisher == null) return BadRequest();
```

10. Now add the request body data below with an *Established* year that is lower than the lowest acceptable value and click the **Send** button. This should trigger the code below and return a *400 Bad Request* status code with the following message in the response body: *The oldest publishing house was founded in 1534.* Check the **Publishers** table to verify that no publisher was added.
Body data:
```
{
        "Name": "Publishing House 4",
        "Established": "1210"
}
```

Code triggered in the **Post** action:
```
if (publisher.Established < 1534)
    ModelState.AddModelError("Established",
        "The oldest publishing house was founded in 1534.");
```

11. Fetch all publishers like you did in the *Fetching All Publishers* section and verify that the no new publisher is returned in the array.

Updating a Publisher

To update a publisher, the **UpdatePublisher** method in the **BookstoreSqlRepository** service class is called from the **Put** action in the **PublishersController** class:

1. Enter the following URL: *http://localhost:55098/api/publishers/3*
2. Fetch the latest publisher with Postman, the one you added. The following data should be returned:
   ```
   {
       "id": 3,
       "name": "Publishing House 3",
       "established": 2017,
       "bookCount": 0,
       "books": []
   }
   ```
3. Select **PUT** in Postman's drop-down.
4. Make sure that the *Content-Type* key is assigned *application/json* in the **Headers** section.
5. Enter the publisher's data in the request **Body** section.
   ```
   {
           "Name": "Publishing House 4",
           "Established": "2016"
   }
   ```
6. Click the **Send** button.
7. A *204 No Content* response status code is returned without any data.
8. Open the **Publishers** table in the database and verify that the publisher was updated. you can click the **Refresh** button above the table data if the table already is open.

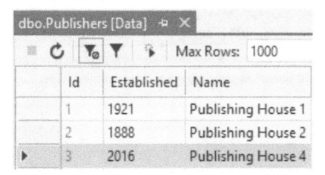

9. Fetch all publishers like you did in the *Fetching All Publishers* section and verify that the altered data for the publisher is returned in the array.

10. Now select **PUT**, remove the request body data, and click the **Send** button again to try to update a publisher without data. This should trigger the code below and return a *400 Bad Request* status code. Check the **Publishers** table to verify that no publisher was altered.
```
if (publisher == null) return BadRequest();
```

11. Now add the body data below with an *Established* year that is lower than the lowest acceptable value and click the **Send** button again. This should trigger the code below and return a *400 Bad Request* status code with the following message in the response body: *The oldest publishing house was founded in 1534.* Check the **Publishers** table to verify that no publisher was added.

    Body data:
```
{
        "Name": "Publishing House 4",
        "Established": "1210"
}
```

    Code triggered in the **Post** action:
```
if (publisher.Established < 1534)
    ModelState.AddModelError("Established",
        "The oldest publishing house was founded in 1534.");
```

12. Change the URI's publisher id to an id that doesn't exist and change the *established* year back to 2016 in the request body.
    http://localhost:55098/api/publishers/3000

13. Click the **Send** button. The response should be a *404 Not Found* status code because the following code is executed.
```
var publisherToUpdate = _rep.GetPublisher(id);
if (publisherToUpdate == null) return NotFound();
```

14. Fetch all publishers like you did in the *Fetching All Publishers* section and verify that the no publisher has been updated by your error handling calls.

Partially Updating a Publisher

To partially update a publisher, the **UpdatePublisher** method in the **BookstoreSqlReposi-tory** service class is called from the **Patch** action in the **PublishersController** class:

1. Enter the following URL: *http://localhost:55098/api/publishers/3*
2. Fetch the latest publisher with Postman, the one you updated. The following data should be returned:

```
{
    "id": 3,
    "name": "Publishing House 4",
    "established": 2016,
    "bookCount": 0,
    "books": []
}
```

3. Select **PATCH** in Postman's drop-down.
4. Make sure that the *Content-Type* key is assigned *application/json* in the **Headers** section.
5. Enter the publisher's data in the request **Body** section.

```
[
    {
        "op": "replace",
        "path":"/name",
        "value": "Patched Publisher"
    }
]
```

6. Click the **Send** button.
7. A *204 No Content* response status code is returned without any data.
8. Open the **Publishers** table in the database and verify that the publisher's name was updated. You can click the **Refresh** button above the table data if the table already is open.

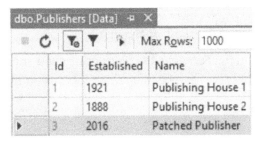

153

9. Fetch all publishers like you did in the *Fetching All Publishers* section and verify that the altered data for the publisher is returned in the array.

10. Now select **PATCH**, remove the body data, and click the **Send** button again to try to update a publisher without data. This should trigger the code below and return a *400 Bad Request* status code. Check the **Publishers** table to verify that no publisher was added.
```
if (publisher == null) return BadRequest();
```

11. Now add the body data below with an *Established* year that is lower than the lowest acceptable value and click the **Send** button again. This should trigger the code below and return a *400 Bad Request* status code with the following message in the response body: *The oldest publishing house was founded in 1534.* Check the **Publishers** table to verify that no publisher was added.
Body data:
```
[
    {
        "op": "replace",
        "path":"/established",
        "value": "1000"
    }
]
```

Code triggered in the **Post** action:
```
if (publisher.Established < 1534)
    ModelState.AddModelError("Established",
        "The oldest publishing house was founded in 1534.");
```

12. Change the URI's publisher id to an id that doesn't exist and change the *established* year back to 2016 in the request body.
http://localhost:55098/api/publishers/3000

13. Click the **Send** button. The response should be a *404 Not Found* status code because the following code is executed.
```
var publisherToUpdate = _rep.GetPublisher(id);
if (publisherToUpdate == null) return NotFound();
```

14. Fetch all publishers like you did in the *Fetching All Publishers* section and verify in the **Publishers** table that no publishers have been updated by your error handling calls.

Deleting a Publisher

To delete a publisher, the **DeletePublisher** method in the **BookstoreSqlRepository** service class is called from the **Delete** action in the **PublishersController** class:

1. Enter the following URL: *http://localhost:55098/api/publishers/3*
2. Fetch the latest publisher with Postman, the one you updated. The following data should be returned:

    ```
    {
        "id": 3,
        "name": "Patched Publisher",
        "established": 2016,
        "bookCount": 0,
        "books": []
    }
    ```

3. Open the **Publishers** table in the database to see the publishers. You can click the **Refresh** button above the table data if the table already is open.

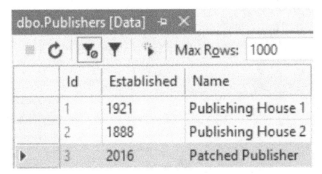

4. Open the **Books** table in the database and make sure that there are books related to the publisher. Add at least one book to the publisher if it doesn't have any books related to it. You can click the **Refresh** button above the table data if the table already is open.

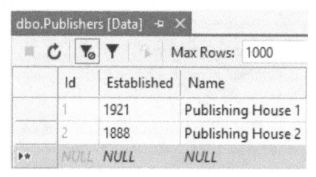

5. Select **DELETE** in Postman's drop-down.
6. Click the **Send** button. This should delete the publisher and its related books in the **Books** table in the database and a *204 No Content* status code should be returned. The books are removed because *cascading delete* is the default setting in EF.
7. Open the **Publishers** table in the database to see the publishers. You can click the **Refresh** button above the table data if the table already is open.

Id	Established	Name
1	1921	Publishing House 1
2	1888	Publishing House 2
NULL	NULL	NULL

8. Open the **Books** table in the database to see the books and make sure that the books related to the deleted publisher have been removed. You can click the **Refresh** button above the table data if the table already is open.

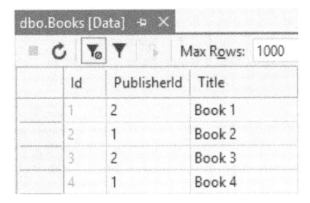

9. Click the **Send** button again to try to remove the already deleted publisher using the same URL as before. The response should be a *404 Not Found* status code because the following code is executed.

```
var publisherToUpdate = _rep.GetPublisher(id);
if (publisherToUpdate == null) return NotFound();
```

Fetching All Books Related to a Publisher

To fetch all books related to a publisher, the **GetBooks** method in the **BookstoreSqlRepository** service class is called through the **Get** action in the **BooksController** class:

1. Enter the following URL: *http://localhost:55098/api/publishers/1/books*
2. Select **GET** in Postman's drop-down.
3. Click the **Send** button.
4. A *200 OK* response status code is returned along with an array of books from the **Books** table.

```
[
    {
        "id": 2,
        "title": "Book 2",
        "publisherId": 1
    },
    {
        "id": 4,
        "title": "Book 4",
        "publisherId": 1
    }
]
```

Fetching a Specific Book Related to a Publisher

To fetch a specific book related to a publisher, the **GetBook** method in the **BookstoreSqlRepository** service class is called through the **Get** action in the **BooksController** class:

1. Enter the following URL: *http://localhost:55098/api/publishers/1/books/2*
2. Select **GET** in Postman's drop-down.
3. Click the **Send** button.
4. A *200 OK* response status code is returned along with the desired book from the **Books** table.
   ```
   {
       "id": 2,
       "title": "Book 2",
       "publisherId": 1
   }
   ```

Fetching a Non-Existing Book

Call the **GetBook** method in the **BookstoreSqlRepository** service class with the **Get** action in the **BooksController** class:

1. URL: *http://localhost:55098/api/publishers/1/books/1000*
2. Select **GET** in Postman's drop-down.
3. Click the **Send** button.
4. A *404 Not Found* response status code is returned because the **Books** table doesn't contain a book with id 1000 related to a publisher with id 1. It's the following code in the **Get** action that triggered the error because the **GetBook** method that tried to fetch the book returned **null**.
   ```
   var book = _rep.GetBook(publisherId, id);
   if (book == null) return NotFound();
   ```

Adding a Book

To add a book, the **AddBook** method in the **BookstoreSqlRepository** service class is called through the **Post** action in the **BooksController** class:

1. Enter the following URL: *http://localhost:55098/api/publishers/1/books*
2. Select **POST** in Postman's drop-down.
3. Make sure that the *Content-Type* key is assigned *application/json* in the **Headers** section.

4. Enter the book's data in the request **Body** section.

```
{
        "title": "New Title"
}
```

5. Click the **Send** button.
6. A *201 Created* response status code is returned along with the added book.
7. Open the **Books** table in the database and verify that the book was added. You can click the **Refresh** button above the table data if the table already is open.

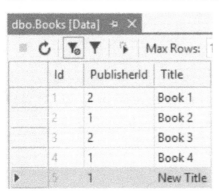

8. Fetch all books like you did in the *Fetching All Books related to a Publisher* section and verify that the new book is returned in the array.
9. Now change the publisher id in the URI to a publisher that doesn't exist: http://localhost:55098/api/publishers/1000/books.
10. Click the **Send** button to try to add a book to a non-existing publisher. This should trigger the code below and return a *404 Not Found* status code. Check the **Books** table to verify that no book was added.
    ```
    var publisherExists = _rep.PublisherExists(publisherId);
    if (!publisherExists) return NotFound();
    ```

11. Now remove the body data and click the **Send** button again to try to add a book without data. This should trigger the code below and return a *400 Bad Request* status code. Check the **Books** table to verify that no book was added.
    ```
    if (book == null) return BadRequest();
    ```

12. Change the publisher id back to *1* in the URI and fetch all books like you did in the *Fetching All Books related to a Publisher* section. Verify that no new book is returned in the array, apart from the one that you added successfully.

Updating a Book

To update a book, the **UpdateBook** method in the **BookstoreSqlRepository** service class is called from the **Put** action in the **BooksController** class:

1. Enter the following URL: *http://localhost:55098/api/publishers/1/books/5*
2. Fetch the latest book with Postman, the one you added. The following data should be returned:
   ```
   {
       "id": 5,
       "title": "New Title",
       "publisherId": 1
   }
   ```
3. Select **PUT** in Postman's drop-down.
4. Make sure that the *Content-Type* key is assigned *application/json* in the **Headers** section.
5. Enter the book data in the request **Body** section.
   ```
   {
       "title": "Altered Title",
       "publisherId": 1
   }
   ```
6. Click the **Send** button.
7. A *204 No Content* response status code is returned without any data.
8. Open the **Books** table in the database and verify that the book was updated. You can click the **Refresh** button above the table data if the table already is open.

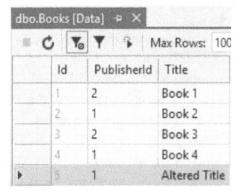

9. Fetch all books like you did in the *Fetching All Books related to a Publisher* section and verify that the altered data for the book is returned in the array.

10. Now select **PUT**, remove the body data, and click the **Send** button again to try to update a book without data. This should trigger the code below and return a *400 Bad Request* status code. Check the **Books** table to verify that no book was added.
    ```
    if (book == null) return BadRequest();
    ```

11. Change the URI's publisher id to an id that doesn't exist. Undo deleting the request body data, or add it again.
    http://localhost:55098/api/publishers/1000/books/5

12. Click the **Send** button. The response should be a *404 Not Found* status code because the following code is executed.
    ```
    var bookToUpdate = _rep.GetBook(publisherId, id);
    if (bookToUpdate == null) return NotFound();
    ```

13. Change the URI's book id to an id that doesn't exist and the publisher id to an existing publisher.
    http://localhost:55098/api/publishers/1/books/5000

14. Click the **Send** button to try to update a non-existing book. The response should be a *404 Not Found* status code because the following code is executed.
    ```
    var bookToUpdate = _rep.GetBook(publisherId, id);
    if (bookToUpdate == null) return NotFound();
    ```

15. Fetch all books like you did in the *Fetching All Books related to a Publisher* section and verify in the **Books** table that the no book has been updated by your error handling calls.

Partially Updating a Book

To partially update a book, the **UpdateBook** method in the **BookstoreSqlRepository** service class is called from the **Patch** action in the **BooksController** class:

1. Enter the following URL: *http://localhost:55098/api/publishers/1/books/5*
2. Fetch the latest book with Postman, the one you updated. The following data should be returned:
   ```
   {
       "id": 5,
       "title": "Altered Title",
       "publisherId": 1
   }
   ```

3. Select **PATCH** in Postman's drop-down.
4. Make sure that the *Content-Type* key is assigned *application/json* in the **Headers** section.
5. Enter the publisher's data in the request **Body** section.

```
[
    {
        "op": "replace",
        "path":"/title",
        "value": "Patched Book"
    }
]
```

6. Click the **Send** button.
7. A *204 No Content* response status code is returned without any data.
8. Open the **Books** table in the database and verify that the book's title was updated. You can click the **Refresh** button above the table data if the table already is open.

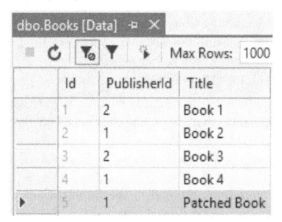

Id	PublisherId	Title
1	2	Book 1
2	1	Book 2
3	2	Book 3
4	1	Book 4
5	1	Patched Book

9. Fetch all books like you did in the *Fetching All Books related to a Publisher* section and verify that the altered data for the book is returned in the array.
10. Change the URI's publisher id to an id that doesn't exist.
    http://localhost:55098/api/publishers/1000/books/5

11. Click the **Send** button to try to update a book that doesn't belong to the specified publisher. The response should be a *404 Not Found* status code because the following code is executed.
    ```
    var bookToUpdate = _rep.GetBook(publisherId, id);
    if (bookToUpdate == null) return NotFound();
    ```

12. Change the URI's book id to an id that doesn't exist and the publisher id to an existing publisher.
    http://localhost:55098/api/publishers/1/books/5000

13. Click the **Send** button to try to update a non-existing book. The response should be a *404 Not Found* status code because the following code is executed.
    ```
    var bookToUpdate = _rep.GetBook(publisherId, id);
    if (bookToUpdate == null) return NotFound();
    ```

14. Fetch all books like you did in the *Fetching All Books related to a Publisher* section and verify that no book has been updated by your error handling calls.

Deleting a Book

To delete a book, the **DeleteBook** method in the **BookstoreSqlRepository** service class is called from the **Delete** action in the **BooksController** class:

1. Enter the following URL: *http://localhost:55098/api/publishers/1/books/5*
2. Fetch the latest book with Postman, the one you updated. The following data should be returned:
    ```
    {
        "id": 5,
        "title": "Patched Book",
        "publisherId": 1
    }
    ```

3. Open the **Books** table in the database to see the books. You can click the **Refresh** button above the table data if the table already is open.

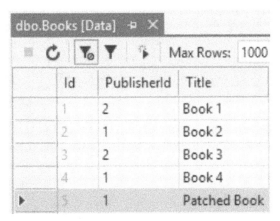

4. Select **DELETE** in Postman's drop-down.

5. Click the **Send** button. This should delete the publisher from the database and a *204 No Content* status code should be returned.
6. Open the **Books** table in the database to see the books. You can click the **Refresh** button above the table data if the table already is open.

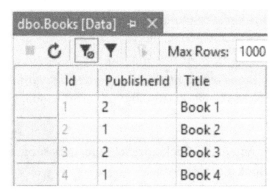

Id	PublisherId	Title
1	2	Book 1
2	1	Book 2
3	2	Book 3
4	1	Book 4

7. Click the **Send** button again to try to remove the book you just deleted, using the same URL as before. The response should be a *404 Not Found* status code because the following code is executed.
```
var book = _rep.GetBook(publisherId, id);
if (book == null) return NotFound();
```

Summary

In this chapter, you installed Entity Framework using the NuGet Package Manager and User Secrets using the *.csproj* file.

You also installed AutoMapper, which you used to map database entity objects to Data Transfer Objects (DTOs).

You also added a **DbContext** class that communicates with the database, and a new database service component class that implements the **IBookstoreRepository** Interface, as a separation between the **DbContext** and the application.

Finally, you added and updated publishers and books in the database. You used Postman to call actions in the two controller classes, that then in turn called methods in the **BookstoreSqlRepository** service class.

Part 4:
Creating a Generic Entity
Framework Service

11. Adding a Generic EF Data Service

Introduction

Wouldn't it be nice if there was a way to create a reusable service that can handle most Entity Framework scenarios with minimal coding? Well, there is. With generics, you can write type safe code, where the current type is assigned when the code is executed. Type safe means that a type can't be changed once the type has been assigned, and by extension, it means that only objects or values of the assigned type can be stored in the variable or collection.

In this chapter, you will create generic methods for interacting with the database. Using generics can minimize the code you need to write since you don't have to write one method for each scenario. Let's use adding entities as an example. In the previous code you added **AddPublisher** and **AddBook** methods to create new entities. That's fine in a small scenario like this, but what if your database has hundreds of tables? That would mean hundreds of methods, just for adding entities.

With generics, you can create one **Add<TEntity>** method that can add an entity to any table. Generics is a way to postpone specifying the type to be used until the instance of the class is created or the method is called.

I'm certain that you have used generics before, even if you didn't know it at the time. One example of applied generics is when you constrain a collection to a specific type with the **<T>** syntax, where **T** is substituted with the actual type you want to use with the collection.

Reflection will be used in a scenario where you fetch books related to a publisher. Reflection is a way to inspect a data type to determine what it contains. You will use reflection to find all related tables to the **TEntity** object sent into the method. In other words, you will find all tables related to a specific table to get its related data; all books related to a publisher.

When creating generic methods, the type of **TEntity** can often be inferred by the object passed into the method, for instance when adding an item to a database.

The interface definition for the **Add** method would look like this:

```
void Add<TEntity>(TEntity item) where TEntity : class;
```

And the method in the service class would look like this:

```
public void Add<TEntity>(TEntity item) where TEntity : class { ... }
```

When calling the **Add** method you could either be explicit and state the type or let the type be inferred by the item passed into the method. Because both the defining type and the passed-in type are the same, .NET Core can figure out the defining type.

If, on the other hand, no object is passed into the method, then the type has to be explicitly defined. Scenarios where defining the type explicitly are: fetching an entity or a list of entities in the **Get** actions.

```
var item = new Publisher();
```

Explicit: `service.Add<Publisher>(item);`

Inferred: `service.Add(item);`

Creating the Generic Service and the Controller classes

You can glean information about the methods needed in the generic interface by looking at the already implemented **IBookstoreRepository**. As you can see, methods for fetching, adding, updating, and deleting entities must be added, as well as the two methods: **Save** and **Exists**. Because you are using generic method definitions, you only need to define one of each method.

The methods must also be restricted to only work on classes because entities are always defined by classes. If the methods aren't restricted, you could, by mistake, use them on value types such as **int** or **long**, which would throw an exception.

You will implement the new interface **IGenericEFRepository** in a service class named **GenericEFRepository**.

1. Add a new interface named **IGenericEFRepository** to the *Services* folder.
2. Add the **public** access modifier to the interface.
   ```
   public interface IGenericEFRepository
   {
   }
   ```
3. Add a new class named **GenericEFRepository** to the *Services* folder.

4. Add the **IGenericEFRepository** interface to the class.
```
public class GenericEFRepository : IGenericEFRepository
{
}
```

5. Add a class-level variable called **_db** of type **SqlDbContext** to the class.
```
private SqlDbContext _db;
```

6. Add a constructor to the service class and inject the **SqlDbContext** into it. Store the injected object in the **_db** variable to make the database accessible in the service.
```
public GenericEFRepository(SqlDbContext db)
{
    _db = db;
}
```

7. Add a scoped service for the interface and the class to the **ConfigureServices** method in the **Startup** class to make it possible to inject it into the controller's constructor.
```
services.AddScoped(typeof(IGenericEFRepository),
    typeof(GenericEFRepository));
```

8. Add a class named **GenPublishersController** to the *Controllers* folder. The controller will handle publisher requests and the generic service handles the data.

9. Inherit the **Controller** class to give it basic controller capabilities.
```
public class GenPublishersController : Controller
{
}
```

10. Add the **Route** attribute to the controller class and assign it the route: *api/genpublishers*.
```
[Route("api/genpublishers")]
```

11. Add a class-level variable called **_rep** of type **IGenericEFRepository** to the class. This variable will hold the service instance passed-in to the constructor.
```
IGenericEFRepository _rep;
```

12. Add a constructor and inject the interface to it. Store the injected object in the **_rep** variable to make it accessible in the controller.

```
public GenPublishersController(IGenericEFRepository rep)
{
    _rep = rep;
}
```

13. Copy the **GenPublishersController** in the *Controllers* folder and paste it into the same folder. Rename the file copy **GenBooksController**. This controller will handle book requests and the generic service will handle book data.

14. Rename the class **GenBooksController** in the renamed file.

The code in the **IGenericEFRepository** interface, so far:

```
public interface IGenericEFRepository
{
}
```

The code in the **GenericEFRepository** service class, so far:

```
public class GenericEFRepository : IGenericEFRepository
{
    private SqlDbContext _db;
    public GenericEFRepository(SqlDbContext db)
    {
        _db = db;
    }
}
```

The code in the **GenPublishersController** class, so far:

```
[Route("api/genpublishers")]
public class GenPublishersController : Controller
{
    IGenericEFRepository _rep;

    public GenPublishersController(IGenericEFRepository rep)
    {
        _rep = rep;
    }
}
```

The code in the **GenBooksController** class, so far:

```
[Route("api/genpublishers")]
public class GenBooksController : Controller
{
    IGenericEFRepository _rep;

    public GenBooksController(IGenericEFRepository rep)
    {
        _rep = rep;
    }
}
```

The complete code in the **ConfigureServices** method in the **Startup** class:

```
public void ConfigureServices(IServiceCollection services)
{
    services.AddMvc();

    var conn = Configuration["connectionStrings:sqlConnection"];
    services.AddDbContext<SqlDbContext>(options =>
        options.UseSqlServer(conn));

    services.AddScoped(typeof(IBookstoreRepository),
        typeof(BookstoreSqlRepository));

    services.AddScoped(typeof(IGenericEFRepository),
        typeof(GenericEFRepository));
}
```

Summary

In this chapter, you began implementing the generic service that will fetch data from an SQL Server database using Entity Framework Core. You also added the **GenBooksController** and **GenPublishersController** classes that will receive the requests from Postman.

12. Implementing the Generic Service

Introduction

In this chapter, you will add method definitions to the **IGenericEFRepository** interface and implement them in the **GenericEFRepository** service. Then you will call the service's methods from the action method's in the **GenPublishersController** class.

Because the methods will be generic in the service, **TEntity** can represent any class. In this scenario, **TEntity** will be replaced by the two entity classes: **Publisher** and **Book**. When either class is defining the method type, that class will be used to manipulate the content of the **DbSet** defining the entity. In other words, if the **Book** class is defining the method, a book will be fetched, added, updated, or deleted from the **Books** table in the database.

Since EF tracks all changes made to existing entities, an **Update** method isn't needed in the service.

The method types must be restricted to only allow classes because an entity must be a class. You restrict a generic method's type by using the **where** keyword.

Method definition in the interface:

```
void Add<TEntity>(TEntity item) where TEntity : class;
```

Method implementation in the service class:

```
public void Add<TEntity>(TEntity item) where TEntity : class
{ ... }
```

You need to add **using** statements for the following namespaces in the controller classes:

```
using AspNetCorePublisherWebAPI.Entities;
using AspNetCorePublisherWebAPI.Models;
using AspNetCorePublisherWebAPI.Services;
using AutoMapper;
using Microsoft.AspNetCore.Mvc;
using System.Collections.Generic;
using System.Linq;
```

The Get<TEntity> Method (Collection)

This method will be able to fetch a collection of publishers or books from either the **Publishers** and **Books** tables as well as data from any future tables.

The generic **TEntity** type will determine which table the data is fetched from. The type will be assigned when the method is called from the controllers, and **TEntity** will be determined at run-time when the method is executed.

Adding the Get<TEntity> Method to the Service

1. Open the **IGenericEFRepository** interface.
2. Add a generic **Get<TEntity>** method that is restricted to only allow classes to represent the **TEntity** type.
   ```
   IEnumerable<TEntity> Get<TEntity>() where TEntity : class;
   ```

3. Open the **GenericEFRepository** class and implement the **Get** method. You can hover over the interface name and use the lightbulb button.
   ```
   public IEnumerable<TEntity> Get<TEntity>() where TEntity : class
   {
       throw new NotImplementedException();
   }
   ```

4. Remove the **throw** statement.
5. You can use the **Set** method on the injected **SqlDbContext** instance to return all the data in the table matching the entity class defining the method.
   ```
   return _db.Set<TEntity>();
   ```

The complete code for the **Get<TEntity>** method:

```
public IEnumerable<TEntity> Get<TEntity>() where TEntity : class
{
    return _db.Set<TEntity>();
}
```

Fetching all Publishers (GET)

1. Open the **GenPublishersController** class.
2. Add a **Get** action decorated with the **[HttpGet]** attribute.
   ```
   [HttpGet]
   public IActionResult Get() { ... }
   ```
3. Fetch the publishers from the database by calling the **Get** method in the service class. Store the publishers in a variable called **items**.
   ```
   var items = _rep.Get<Publisher>();
   ```
4. Use AutoMapper to convert the entity objects to instances of the **PublisherDTO** class and return the collection.
   ```
   var DTOs = Mapper.Map<IEnumerable<PublisherDTO>>(items);
   return Ok(DTOs);
   ```
5. Save all files.
6. Place a breakpoint in the **Get** action in the **GenPublishersController** class to make sure that the action is executed when Postman calls the Web API.
7. Run the application (F5) and open Postman.
8. Select **GET** in Postman's drop-down.
9. Enter the URL to the **Get** action and click the **Send** button.
   *http://localhost:55098/api/**gen**publishers*
10. The execution should stop at the breakpoint. Press F5 to continue. The following response body should be returned from the database.
    ```
    [
        {
            "id": 1,
            "name": "Publishing House 1",
            "established": 1921,
            "bookCount": 0,
            "books": []
        },
        {
            "id": 2,
            "name": "Publishing House 2",
            "established": 1888,
            "bookCount": 0,
            "books": []
        }
    ]
    ```

11. Close browser to stop the application.
12. Remove the breakpoint.

The complete code for the **Get** action in the **GenPublishersController** class:

```
[HttpGet]
public IActionResult Get()
{
    var item = _rep.Get<Publisher>();
    var DTOs = Mapper.Map<IEnumerable<PublisherDTO>>(item);
    return Ok(DTOs);
}
```

Fetching all Books (GET)

1. Open the **GenPublishersController** class.
2. Copy the **Get** action you just added.
3. Open the **GenBooksController** class.
4. Paste in the copied **Get** action below the constructor.
5. Add the *{publisherId}/books* URI to the **[HttpGet]** attribute.
   `[HttpGet("{publisherId}/books")]`

6. Add a parameter named **publisherId (int)** to the action method definition so that the action can receive the desired publisher's id to filter the result based on that id.
   ```
   public IActionResult Get(int publisherId)
   {
   }
   ```

7. Change the defining type to **Book** for the **Get** method and use the **Where** LINQ method to fetch only books related to the publisher matching the passed-in id.
   ```
   var items = _rep.Get<Book>().Where(b =>
       b.PublisherId.Equals(publisherId));
   ```

8. Change the **PublisherDTO** type to **BookDTO** in the AutoMapper conversion.
   ```
   var DTOs = Mapper.Map<IEnumerable<BookDTO>>(items);
   ```

9. Save all files.
10. Place a breakpoint in the **Get** action in the **GenBooksController** class.
11. Run the application (F5) and open Postman.
12. Select **GET** in Postman's drop-down.
13. Enter the URL to the **Get** action and click the **Send** button.

http://localhost:55098/api/genpublishers/1/books

14. The execution should stop at the breakpoint. Press F5 to continue. The following response body should be returned from the database.

```
[
    {
        "id": 2,
        "title": "Book 2",
        "publisherId": 1
    },
    {
        "id": 4,
        "title": "Book 4",
        "publisherId": 1
    }
]
```

15. Close the browser to stop the application.
16. Remove the breakpoint.

The complete code for the **Get** action in the **GenBooksController** class:

```
[HttpGet("{publisherId}/books")]
public IActionResult Get(int publisherId)
{
    var items = _rep.Get<Book>().Where(b =>
        b.PublisherId.Equals(publisherId));

    var DTOs = Mapper.Map<IEnumerable<BookDTO>>(items);
    return Ok(DTOs);
}
```

The Get<TEntity> Method (One)

This method will be able to fetch a single publisher or book from either the **Publishers** or **Books** tables, as well as from any future tables.

The generic **TEntity** type will determine which table the data is fetched from. The type will be assigned when calling the method from the controllers and **TEntity** will be determined at run-time when the method is executed.

You will use reflection to fetch the records related to the parent record (books related to a publisher). Reflection makes it possible to examine a type to see what it contains. In this scenario, you will use it to find out what related entity the **Publisher** class has by comparing its properties with the **DbSets** in the **SqlDbContext**. When the related tables (**DbSets**) have been found, the data related to the publisher is loaded into its entity properties. In this case the **ICollection<Book>** property in the **Publisher** object will be filled with data.

There are six steps to achieving this:

1. Fetch the parent record from the database.
2. Check if the record exists and the **includeRelatedEntities** parameter is **true**.
3. If step 2 is true, then:
   a. List the names of all the **DbSet** properties in the **SqlDbContext**.
   b. List the names of all the entity properties in the parent type by comparing the **DbSet** property type names with the type names in the parent type. This will give you all the properties that use an entity class.
   c. If there are property names in the list from step b then iterate over the found entities (**DbSets**) and load their data in the parent record.
4. Return the fetched data.

You need to add **using** statements to the following namespaces:

```
using System.Reflection;
using System.Linq;
```

Adding the Get<TEntity> Method to the Service

1. Open the **IGenericEFRepository** interface.
2. Add a generic **Get<TEntity>** method that is restricted to only allow classes to represent the **TEntity** type and it must have two parameters: **id (int)** and **includeRelatedEntities (bool)** that determines if the related records should be returned with the parent record; for example, books related to a publisher.
   ```
   TEntity Get<TEntity>(int id, bool includeRelatedEntities = false)
   where TEntity : class;
   ```
3. Open the **GenericEFRepository** class and implement the **Get** method. You can hover over the interface name and use the lightbulb button.
   ```
   public TEntity Get<TEntity>(int id, bool includeRelatedEntities =
   false) where TEntity : class
   {
       throw new NotImplementedException();
   }
   ```

4. Remove the **throw** statement.

5. Fetch the parent record with the passed-in id using the **Set** method on the database context combined with the **Find** LINQ method.
```
var entity = _db.Set<TEntity>().Find(new object[] { id });
```

6. Check if the record exists and the **includeRelatedEntities** parameter is **true**.
```
if (entity != null && includeRelatedEntities)
{
}
```

7. Fetch the property names of all the **DbSets** in the **SqlDbContext** (the table names) and store them in a variable named **dbsets**.
```
var dbsets = typeof(SqlDbContext)
    .GetProperties(BindingFlags.Public | BindingFlags.Instance)
    .Where(z => z.PropertyType.Name.Contains("DbSet"))
    .Select(z => z.Name);
```

8. Fetch the names of all properties in the generic type **TEntity** that are represented by a **DbSet** in the **SqlDbContext**. Store the table names in a variable called **tables**.
```
var tables = typeof(TEntity)
    .GetProperties(BindingFlags.Public | BindingFlags.Instance)
    .Where(z => dbsets.Contains(z.Name))
    .Select(z => z.Name);
```

9. Load data into all the tables referenced by the parent type (**TEntity**).
```
if (tables.Count() > 0)
    foreach (var table in tables)
        _db.Entry(entity).Collection(table).Load();
```

10. Return the **entity** variable outside the if-block.
```
return entity;
```

11. Save all files.

The complete code for the **Get<TEntity>** method:
```
public TEntity Get<TEntity>(int id, bool includeRelatedEntities = false)
where TEntity : class
{
    var entity = _db.Set<TEntity>().Find(new object[] { id });
```

```
if (entity != null && includeRelatedEntities)
    {
        // Get the names of all DbSets in the DbContext
        var dbsets = typeof(SqlDbContext)
            .GetProperties(BindingFlags.Public | BindingFlags.Instance)
            .Where(z => z.PropertyType.Name.Contains("DbSet"))
            .Select(z => z.Name);

        // Get the names of all the properties (tables) in the generic
        // type T that is represented by a DbSet
        var tables = typeof(TEntity)
            .GetProperties(BindingFlags.Public | BindingFlags.Instance)
            .Where(z => dbsets.Contains(z.Name))
            .Select(z => z.Name);

        // Eager load all the tables referenced by the generic type T
        if (tables.Count() > 0)
            foreach (var table in tables)
                _db.Entry(entity).Collection(table).Load();
    }

    return entity;
}
```

Fetching One Publisher (GET)

1. Open the **GenPublishersController** class.
2. Add a second **Get** method and decorate it with the **[HttpGet]** attribute. The attribute URI should contain *{id}* representing the publisher's id and be named **GetGenericPublisher**; you name it so that you can reuse it later. The action method should have two parameters: **id (int)** and **includeRelatedEntities (bool)**. The latter parameter determines whether related records should be loaded (the books related to a publisher).
   ```
   [HttpGet("{id}", Name = "GetGenericPublisher")]
   public IActionResult Get(int id, bool includeRelatedEntities = false)
   ```
3. Fetch the publisher matching the passed-in id and store the result in a variabale named **item**.
   ```
   var item = _rep.Get<Publisher>(id, includeRelatedEntities);
   ```
4. Return a *404 Not Found* status code if no matching publisher was found.
   ```
   if (item == null) return NotFound();
   ```

5. Convert the publisher into a **PublisherDTO** object and return it.

```
var DTO = Mapper.Map<PublisherDTO>(item);
return Ok(DTO);
```

6. Start the application and open Postman.

7. Select **GET** in Postman's drop-down.

8. Enter the following two URLs (one at a time). They should return the same response body when the **Send** button is clicked. It's important that there are no spaces in the URL.

   http://localhost:55098/api/genpublishers/1
   *http://localhost:55098/api/genpublishers/1?includeRelatedEntities=**false***

   Result:

```
{
    "id": 1,
    "name": "Publishing House 1",
    "established": 1921,
    "bookCount": 0,
    "books": []
}
```

9. Change *false* to *true* in the URL and click the **Send** button again. Thanks to the reflection you added, this should return the publisher and its related books. It's important that there are no spaces in the URL.

   *http://localhost:55098/api/genpublishers/1?includeRelatedEntities=**true***

   Result:

```
{
    "id": 1,
    "name": "Publishing House 1",
    "established": 1921,
    "bookCount": 2,
    "books": [
        {
            "id": 2,
            "title": "Book 2",
            "publisherId": 1
        },
        {
            "id": 4,
            "title": "Book 4",
            "publisherId": 1
```

```
        }
    ]
}
```

The complete code in the **Get** action in the **GenPublishersController** class:

```
[HttpGet("{id}", Name = "GetGenericPublisher")]
public IActionResult Get(int id, bool includeRelatedEntities = false)
{
    var item = _rep.Get<Publisher>(id, includeRelatedEntities);

    if (item == null) return NotFound();

    var DTO = Mapper.Map<PublisherDTO>(item);
    return Ok(DTO);
}
```

Fetching One Book (GET)

1. Open the **GenPublishersController** class.
2. Copy the **Get** action method you just added.
3. Open the **GenBooksController** class.
4. Paste in the **Get** action you copied.
5. Change the URI to: *{publisherId}/books/{id}*.
6. Change the name to *GetGenericBook* in the attribute.
   ```
   [HttpGet("{publisherId}/books/{id}", Name = "GetGenericBook")]
   ```
7. Add a **publisherId (int)** parameter to the beginning of the action method's parameter list.
   ```
   public IActionResult Get(int publisherId, int id, bool
   includeRelatedEntities = false)
   ```
8. Change the defining type to **Book** in the generic **Get** method call.
   ```
   var item = _rep.Get<Book>(id, includeRelatedEntities);
   ```
9. Return a 404 Not Found status code if the book wasn't found or if the publisher id in the **publisherId** parameter doesn't match the publisher id in the fetched book.
   ```
   if (item == null || !item.PublisherId.Equals(publisherId)) return
   NotFound();
   ```
10. Change **PublisherDTO** to **BookDTO**.
    ```
    var DTO = Mapper.Map<BookDTO>(item);
    ```

11. Start the application and open Postman.
12. Select **GET** in Postman's drop-down.
13. Enter the URL below and click the **Send** button. There's no point in adding the *includeRelatedEntities* to the URL since the **Books** table has no references to any child tables.
    http://localhost:55098/api/genpublishers/1/books/2
    Result:
    ```
    {
        "id": 2,
        "title": "Book 2",
        "publisherId": 1
    }
    ```

The complete code for the **Get** action in the **GenBooksController** class:

```
[HttpGet("{publisherId}/books/{id}", Name = "GetGenericBook")]
public IActionResult Get(int publisherId, int id, bool
includeRelatedEntities = false)
{
    var item = _rep.Get<Book>(id, includeRelatedEntities);

    if (item == null || !item.PublisherId.Equals(publisherId))
        return NotFound();

    var DTO = Mapper.Map<BookDTO>(item);
    return Ok(DTO);
}
```

The Save Method

This method will persist all changes made to the tables in the **SqlDbContext**. It doesn't need a **TEntity** type since it only calls the **SaveChanges** method on the context, and that method is the same for all entities.

1. Open the **IGenericEFRepository** interface.
2. Add a method named **Save** that takes no parameters and return a **bool** value that specifies if the data was persisted successfully.
   bool Save();

3. Open the **GenericEFRepository** class and implement the **Save** method. You can hover over the interface name and use the lightbulb button.

```
public bool Save()
{
    throw new NotImplementedException();
}
```

4. Remove the **throw** statement.
5. Call the **SaveChanges** method on the **SqlDbContext** and return **true** if the number of rows affected are greater than or equal to zero.
    ```
    return _db.SaveChanges() >= 0;
    ```

The complete code for the **Save** method:

```
public bool Save()
{
    return _db.SaveChanges() >= 0;
}
```

The Add<TEntity> Method

This method will be able to add a single publisher or book to either the **Publishers** or **Books** tables, as well as to any future tables.

The generic **TEntity** type will determine which table the data is added to. The type will be assigned when the method is called from the controllers, and **TEntity** will be determined at run-time when the method is executed.

6. Open the **IGenericEFRepository** interface.
7. Add a generic **Add<TEntity>** method that is restricted to only allow classes to represent the **TEntity** type.
    ```
    void Add<TEntity>(TEntity item) where TEntity : class;
    ```

8. Open the **GenericEFRepository** class and implement the **Add** method. You can hover over the interface name and use the light-bulb button.
    ```
    public void Add<TEntity>(TEntity item) where TEntity : class
    {
        throw new NotImplementedException();
    }
    ```

9. Remove the **throw** statement.
10. You can use the **Add** method on the injected **SqlDbContext** instance to add the data to the table matching the entity class defining the method.
    ```
    _db.Add<TEntity>(item);
    ```

The complete code for the **Add<TEntity>** method:

```
public void Add<TEntity>(TEntity item) where TEntity : class
{
    _db.Add<TEntity>(item);
}
```

Add a Publisher (POST)

1. Open the **GenPublishersController** class.
2. Add a **Post** action decorated with the **[HttpPost]** attribute. The **DTO** (**PublisherDTO**) method parameter should be decorated with the **[FromBody]** to receive data from the request body sent from Postman.
   ```
   [HttpPost]
   public IActionResult Post([FromBody]PublisherDTO DTO)
   {
   }
   ```
3. Return a *400 Bad Request* if the **DTO** parameter is **null** or the model state is invalid.
   ```
   if (DTO == null) return BadRequest();
   if (!ModelState.IsValid) return BadRequest(ModelState);
   ```
4. Use AutoMapper to convert the passed-in **DTO** to a **Publisher** object and store it in a variable called **itemToCreate**.
   ```
   var itemToCreate = Mapper.Map<Publisher>(DTO);
   ```
5. Add the record to the database by calling the **Add** method you just added. Note that you don't explicitly have to specify a type for the **TEntity** type. It's inferred by the object passed-in to the method. EF keeps track of all changes until the **SaveChanges** method on the **SqlDbContext** object is called, which means that you can add, update, and delete several records before saving.
   ```
   _rep.Add(itemToCreate);
   ```
6. Call the **Save** method to persist the changes. Return a *500 Internal Server Error* status code if something goes wrong when saving.
   ```
   if (!_rep.Save()) return StatusCode(500,
       "A problem occurred while handling your request.");
   ```
7. Use AutoMapper to convert the **Publisher** object back to a **PublisherDTO** object and store it in a variable called **createdDTO**.
   ```
   var createdDTO = Mapper.Map<PublisherDTO>(itemToCreate);
   ```

8. Reroute to the **Get** action you named **GetGenericPublisher** by returning a call to the **CreatedAtRoute** method with the necessary data. The first parameter is the name of the action to call, the second is an anonymous object containing values for the action's paramaters, and the last is the added record.
```
return CreatedAtRoute("GetGenericPublisher", new { id =
createdDTO.Id }, createdDTO);
```

9. Save all files.

10. Place a breakpoint in the **Add** action in the **GenPublishersController** class.

11. Run the application (F5) and open Postman.

12. Select **POST** in Postman's drop-down.

13. Enter the URL to the **Add** action.
    http://localhost:55098/api/genpublishers

14. Make sure that the *Content-Type* header has been added and contains the value *application/json*.

15. Add the following publisher data to the request body and click the **Send** button.
```
{
    "name": "Added Publishing House",
    "established": 2018
}
```

16. The execution should stop at the breakpoint. Press F5 to continue. The following response body should be returned from the database (the id might be different).
```
{
    "id": 6,
    "name": "Added Publishing House",
    "established": 2018,
    "bookCount": 0,
    "books": []
}
```

17. Close the browser to stop the application.

18. Remove the breakpoint.

The complete code for the **Post** action in the **GenPublishersController** class:

```
[HttpPost]
public IActionResult Post([FromBody]PublisherDTO DTO)
{
    if (DTO == null) return BadRequest();
    if (!ModelState.IsValid) return BadRequest(ModelState);

    var itemToCreate = Mapper.Map<Publisher>(DTO);

    _rep.Add(itemToCreate);

    if (!_rep.Save()) return StatusCode(500,
        "A problem occurred while handling your request.");

    var createdDTO = Mapper.Map<PublisherDTO>(itemToCreate);

    return CreatedAtRoute("GetGenericPublisher",
        new { id = createdDTO.Id }, createdDTO);
}
```

Add a Book (POST)

1. Open the **GenPublishersController** class.
2. Copy the **Post** action method you just added.
3. Open the **GenBooksController** class and paste in the **Post** action you copied.
4. Add the following URI to the **[HttpPost]** attribute: *{publisherId}/books*.
   `[HttpPost("{publisherId}/books")]`
5. Add a **publisherId (int)** parameter to the beginning of the action method's parameter list and change the **PublisherDTO** type to **BookDTO**.
   `public IActionResult Post(int publisherId, [FromBody]BookDTO DTO)`
6. Change the defining type to **Book** in the first AutoMapper conversion.
   `var itemToCreate = Mapper.Map<Book>(DTO);`
7. Change the defining type to **BookDTO** in the second AutoMapper conversion.
   `var createdDTO = Mapper.Map<BookDTO>(itemToCreate);`
8. Assign the value in the *publisherId* URI parameter to the **PublisherId** of the **itemToCreate** object.
   `itemToCreate.PublisherId = publisherId;`
9. Change the action to call in the **CreatedAtRoute** method to *GetGenericBook*.

```
        return CreatedAtRoute("GetGenericBook", new { id = createdDTO.Id
        }, createdDTO);
```

14. Start the application and open Postman.
15. Select **POST** in Postman's drop-down.
16. Enter the URL to the **Post** action.
    http://localhost:55098/api/genpublishers/1/books

17. Make sure that the *Content-Type* header has been added and contains the value *application/json*.
18. Add the following request body and click the **Send** button.
    ```
    { "title": "Added Book" }
    ```

19. The following response body should be returned from the database (the id might be different).
    ```
    {
        "id": 17,
        "title": "Added Book",
        "publisherId": 1
    }
    ```

20. Close the browser to stop the application.

The complete code for the **Post** action in the **GenBooksController** class:

```
[HttpPost("{publisherId}/books")]
public IActionResult Post(int publisherId, [FromBody]BookDTO DTO)
{
    if (DTO == null) return BadRequest();
    if (!ModelState.IsValid) return BadRequest(ModelState);

    var itemToCreate = Mapper.Map<Book>(DTO);
    itemToCreate.PublisherId = publisherId;
    _rep.Add(itemToCreate);

    if (!_rep.Save()) return StatusCode(500,
        "A problem occurred while handling your request.");

    var createdDTO = Mapper.Map<BookDTO>(itemToCreate);

    return CreatedAtRoute("GetGenericBook",
        new { id = createdDTO.Id }, createdDTO);
}
```

Updating an Entity

Since EF tracks all changes made to existing entities, an **Update** method isn't needed in the service. When the DTO passed-in to the action is merged with the fetched entity, EF will track those changes.

When updating an entity, the primary key is never changed. Use the **PublisherUpdateDTO** class for the **DTO** parameter since it hasn't got an **Id** parameter representing the primary key. Use the *{id}* passed-in through the URI to find the record to change.

Updating a Publisher (PUT)

1. Open the **GenPublishersController** class.
2. Add a **Put** action decorated with the **[HttpPut]** attribute, with an *{id}* in the URI. The action should have two parameters: **id (int)** and **DTO (PublisherUpdateDTO)** decorated with the **[FromBody]**.
   ```
   [HttpPut("{id}")]
   public IActionResult Put(int id, [FromBody]PublisherUpdateDTO DTO)
   {
   }
   ```
3. Return a *400 Bad Request* if the **DTO** parameter is **null** or the model state is invalid.
   ```
   if (DTO == null) return BadRequest();
   if (!ModelState.IsValid) return BadRequest(ModelState);
   ```
4. Fetch the publisher to change by calling the **Get** method with the **SqlDbContext** object. Return a *404 Not Found* status code if the publisher wasn't found.
   ```
   var entity = _rep.Get<Publisher>(id);
   if (entity == null) return NotFound();
   ```
5. Use AutoMapper to map the property values from the passed-in **DTO** object with the fetched **Publisher** object stored in the **entity** variable.
   ```
   Mapper.Map(DTO, entity);
   ```
6. Call the **Save** method to persist the changes. Return a *500 Internal Server Error* status code if something goes wrong when saving.
   ```
   if (!_rep.Save()) return StatusCode(500,
       "A problem occurred while handling your request.");
   ```
7. Return a *204 No Content* status code to show that the change was persisted successfully.
8. Open the **Startup** class and locate the **Configure** method.

9. Add mappings to AutoMapper for a **PublisherDTO** to a **Publisher** entity, a **PublisherUpdateDTO** to a **Publisher** entity, and a **BookUpdateDTO** to a **Book** entity. Also, add the reverse mappings.

```
config.CreateMap<Models.PublisherDTO, Entities.Publisher>();
config.CreateMap<Models.PublisherUpdateDTO, Entities.Publisher>();
config.CreateMap<Entities.Publisher, Models.PublisherUpdateDTO>();
config.CreateMap<Models.BookUpdateDTO, Entities.Book>();
config.CreateMap<Entities.Book, Models.BookUpdateDTO>();
```

10. Save all files.

11. Open the **Publishers** table in the database as a reference point before changing any data.

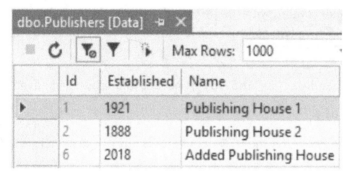

12. Run the application (F5) and open Postman.

13. Select **PUT** in Postman's drop-down.

14. Enter the URL to the **Put** action.

    http://localhost:55098/api/genpublishers/1

15. Make sure that the *Content-Type* header has been added and contains the value *application/json*.

16. Add the following publisher's data to the request body and click the **Send** button.

```
{
    "name": "Updated Publishing House 1",
    "established": 1821
}
```

17. A *204 No Content* status code should be returned to Postman.

18. Close the browser to stop the application.

19. Open the **Publishers** table again and refresh its data.

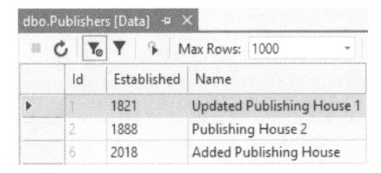

The complete code for the **Put** action in the **GenPublishersController** class:

```
[HttpPut("{id}")]
public IActionResult Put(int id, [FromBody]PublisherUpdateDTO DTO)
{
    if (DTO == null) return BadRequest();
    if (!ModelState.IsValid) return BadRequest(ModelState);

    var entity = _rep.Get<Publisher>(id);
    if (entity == null) return NotFound();

    Mapper.Map(DTO, entity);

    if (!_rep.Save()) return StatusCode(500,
        "A problem happened while handling your request.");

    return NoContent();
}
```

Updating a Book (PUT)

1. Open the **GenPublishersController** class.
2. Copy the **Put** action method you just added.
3. Open the **GenBooksController** class.
4. Paste in the **Put** action you copied.
5. Change the URI in the **[HttpPut]** attribute to: *{publisherId}/books/{id}*.
   ```
   [HttpPut("{publisherId}/books/{id}")]
   ```
6. Add a **publisherId (int)** parameter to the beginning of the action method's parameter list and change the **PublisherUpdateDTO** type to **BookUpdateDTO**.
   ```
   public IActionResult Put(int publisherId, int id,
   [FromBody]BookUpdateDTO DTO)
   ```

7. Change the defining type to **Book** for the **Get** method.
   ```
   var entity = _rep.Get<Book>(id);
   ```

8. Save all files.

9. Open the **Books** table in the database as a reference point before changing any data.

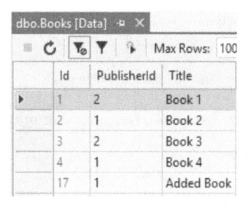

10. Run the application (F5) and open Postman.

11. Select **PUT** in Postman's drop-down.

12. Enter the URL to the **Put** action.
    http://localhost:55098/api/genpublishers/2/books/1

13. Make sure that the *Content-Type* header has been added and contains the value *application/json*.

14. Add the following book data to the request body and click the **Send** button.
    ```
    {
        "title": "Updated Book 1",
        "publisherId": 2
    }
    ```

15. A *204 No Content* status code should have been returned to Postman.

16. Close browser to stop the application.

17. Open the **Books** table again and refresh its data.

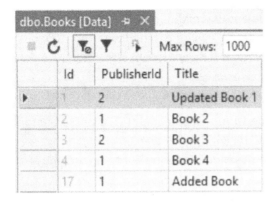

The complete code for the **Put** action in the **GenBooksController** class:

```
[HttpPut("{publisherId}/books/{id}")]
public IActionResult Put(int publisherId, int id,
[FromBody]BookUpdateDTO DTO)
{
    if (DTO == null) return BadRequest();
    if (!ModelState.IsValid) return BadRequest(ModelState);

    var entity = _rep.Get<Book>(id);
    if (entity == null) return NotFound();

    Mapper.Map(DTO, entity);

    if (!_rep.Save()) return StatusCode(500,
        "A problem happened while handling your request.");

    return NoContent();
}
```

Partially Updating a Publisher (PATCH)

1. Open the **GenPublishersController** class.
2. Copy the **Put** action method you just added and paste it in below the **Put** action.
3. Change the attribute to **[HttpPatch]**.
   ```
   [HttpPatch("{id}")]
   ```

4. Change the action name to **Patch** and the **PublisherUpdateDTO** to
   JsonPatchDocument<PublisherUpdateDTO>.
   ```
   public IActionResult Patch(int id,
   [FromBody]JsonPatchDocument<PublisherUpdateDTO> DTO)
   ```

5. Use AutoMapper to convert the entity fetched from the database to a **PublisherUpdateDTO** object so that it can be patched with the DTO passed-in to the action. Add the code below the **if (entity == null)** statement (the new code should not be part of the if statement).
   ```
   var entityToPatch = Mapper.Map<PublisherUpdateDTO>(entity);
   ```

6. Use the **ApplyTo** method on the **JsonPatchDocument** DTO passed-in to the action to patch the data in the DTO with the converted entity in the **entityToPatch** variable. Pass in the **ModelState** object to record any errors that might occur.
   ```
   DTO.ApplyTo(entityToPatch, ModelState);
   ```

7. Call the **TryToValidate** method to see if there are any patch errors and return a *400 Bad Request* status code if errors are present.
   ```
   TryValidateModel(entityToPatch);
   if (!ModelState.IsValid) return BadRequest(ModelState);
   ```

8. Change **DTO** to **entityToPatch** in the second AutoMapper **Map** method.
   ```
   Mapper.Map(entityToPatch, entity);
   ```

9. Save all files.

10. Open the **Publishers** table as a reference point before changing any data.

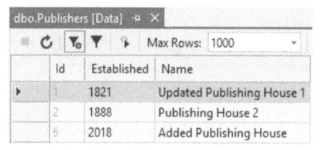

11. Run the application (F5) and open Postman.

12. Select **PATCH** in Postman's drop-down.

13. Enter the URL to the **Patch** action.
    http://localhost:55098/api/genpublishers/1

14. Make sure that the *Content-Type* header has been added and contains the value *application/json*.

15. Add the following request body to change the name of the publishing house and click the **Send** button.
    ```
    [
    ```

```
        {
            "op": "replace",
            "path":"/name",
            "value": "Patched Publishing House 1"
        }
    ]
```

16. A *204 No Content* status code should be returned to Postman.
17. Close browser to stop the application.
18. Open the **Publishers** table again and refresh its data.

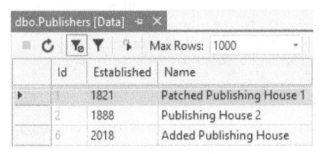

The complete code for the **Patch** action in the **GenPublishersController** class:

```
[HttpPatch("{id}")]
public IActionResult Patch(int id,
[FromBody]JsonPatchDocument<PublisherUpdateDTO> DTO)
{
    if (DTO == null) return BadRequest();
    if (!ModelState.IsValid) return BadRequest(ModelState);

    var entity = _rep.Get<Publisher>(id);
    if (entity == null) return NotFound();

    var entityToPatch = Mapper.Map<PublisherUpdateDTO>(entity);
    DTO.ApplyTo(entityToPatch, ModelState);
    TryValidateModel(entityToPatch);
    if (!ModelState.IsValid) return BadRequest(ModelState);

    Mapper.Map(entityToPatch, entity);

    if (!_rep.Save()) return StatusCode(500,
        "A problem happened while handling your request.");

    return NoContent();
}
```

Partially Updating a Book (PATCH)

1. Open the **GenPublishersController** class.
2. Copy the **Patch** action method you just added.
3. Open the **GenBooksController** class.
4. Paste in the **Patch** action you copied.
5. Change the URI in the **[HttpPatch]** attribute to: *{publisherId}/books/{id}*.
    ```
    [HttpPatch("{publisherId}/books/{id}")]
    ```

6. Add a **publisherId (int)** parameter at the beginning of the action method's parameter list and change the **PublisherUpdateDTO** type to **BookUpdateDTO**.
    ```
    public IActionResult Patch(int publisherId, int id,
    [FromBody]JsonPatchDocument<BookUpdateDTO> DTO)
    ```

7. Change the defining type to **Book** for the **Get** method.
    ```
    var entity = _rep.Get<Book>(id);
    ```

8. Change the **PublisherUpdateDTO** type to **BookUpdateDTO** in the AutoMapper mapping for the **entityToPatch** variable assignment.
    ```
    var entityToPatch = Mapper.Map<BookUpdateDTO>(entity);
    ```

9. Save all files.
10. Open the **Books** table in the database as a reference point before changing any data.

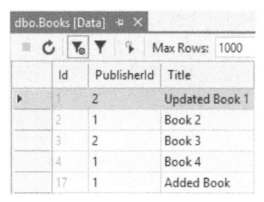

11. Run the application (F5) and open Postman.
12. Select **PATCH** in Postman's drop-down.
13. Enter the URL to the **Patch** action.
    http://localhost:55098/api/genpublishers/2/books/1

14. Make sure that the *Content-Type* header has been added and contains the value *application/json*.

15. Add the following request body data to change the value of the book title, and click the **Send** button.

```
[
    {
        "op": "replace",
        "path":"/title",
        "value": "Patched Title"
    }
]
```

16. A *204 No Content* status code should be returned to Postman.

17. Close the browser to stop the application.

18. Open the **Books** table again and refresh its data.

Id	PublisherId	Title
1	2	Patched Title
2	1	Book 2
3	2	Book 3
4	1	Book 4
17	1	Added Book

The complete code for the **Patch** action in the **GenBooksController** class:

```
[HttpPatch("{publisherId}/books/{id}")]
public IActionResult Patch(int publisherId, int id,
[FromBody]JsonPatchDocument<BookUpdateDTO> DTO)
{
    if (DTO == null) return BadRequest();
    if (!ModelState.IsValid) return BadRequest(ModelState);

    var entity = _rep.Get<Book>(id);
    if (entity == null) return NotFound();

    var entityToPatch = Mapper.Map<BookUpdateDTO>(entity);
    DTO.ApplyTo(entityToPatch, ModelState);
```

```
    TryValidateModel(entityToPatch);
    if (!ModelState.IsValid) return BadRequest(ModelState);

    Mapper.Map(entityToPatch, entity);

    if (!_rep.Save()) return StatusCode(500,
        "A problem happened while handling your request.");

    return NoContent();
}
```

Adding the Exists<TEntity> Method to the Service

This method checks if a record exists in the table defined by **TEntity**.

1. Open the **IGenericEFRepository** interface.
2. Add a method definition for the **Exists<TEntity>** method. Its type should be defined by **TEntity** and it should have one parameter **id** (**int**) that represents the id of the record to check. The method should return a **bool** value.
   ```
   bool Exists<TEntity>(int id) where TEntity : class;
   ```

3. Open the **GenericEFRepository** class.
4. Add the **Exists<TEntity>** method.
5. Remove the **throw** statement.
6. Return **true** if the record exists in the table defined by **TEntity**. Get the entity (table) with the context's **Set** method and use the **Find** LINQ method to try to fetch the record matching the id passed-in to the **Exists** method. Return **true** if the result isn't **null**, because that means that the record exists.
   ```
   return _db.Set<TEntity>().Find(new object[] { id }) != null;
   ```

7. Save all files.

The complete code for the **Exists<TEntity>** method:

```
public bool Exists<TEntity>(int id) where TEntity : class
{
    return _db.Set<TEntity>().Find(new object[] { id }) != null;
}
```

The Delete<TEntity> Method

The **Delete** method will be able to delete a publisher and its related books, or a single book from the **Publishers** and **Books** tables, or records from any future table.

The generic **TEntity** type will determine which table the data is deleted from. The type will be assigned when the method is called from a controller, and **TEntity** will be determined at run-time when the method is executed.

Before deleting a record, you first have to check that it exists. That's where the **Exists** method that you will add comes into the picture. You can check if an entity exists by calling the **Find** LINQ method on the **Set** method.

You will add a **Delete** method (to the service) that deletes a record by calling the **Remove** LINQ method on the **Set** method.

Adding the Delete Method to the Service

This method deletes a record from the table defined by **TEntity**.

IMPORTANT! *By default, EF is configured for cascading delete, which means that all related records will be deleted as well. In other words, if you delete a publisher that has related books, then those books will be removed with the publisher.*

1. Open the **IGenericEFRepository** interface.
2. Add a method definition for the **Delete<TEntity>** method. Its type should be defined by **TEntity** and it should have one parameter **item** (**TEntity**) that represents the record to delete. The method shouldn't return any value.
   ```
   void Delete<TEntity>(TEntity item) where TEntity : class;
   ```
3. Open the **GenericEFRepository** class.
4. Add the **Delete<TEntity>** method.
5. Remove the **throw** statement.
6. Get the entity (table) with the context's **Set** method and use the **Remove** LINQ method to try to delete the **TEntity** record passed-in to the **Delete<TEntity>** method.
   ```
   _db.Set<TEntity>().Remove(item);
   ```
7. Save all files.

The complete code for the **Delete<TEntity>** method:

```
public void Delete<TEntity>(TEntity item) where TEntity : class
{
    _db.Set<TEntity>().Remove(item);
}
```

Deleting a Publisher (DELETE)

1. Open the **GenPublishersController** class.
2. Add a **Delete** action decorated with the **[HttpDelete]** attribute with an *{id}* in the URI. The action should have an **id (int)** parameter.
   ```
   [HttpDelete("{id}")]
   public IActionResult Delete(int id)
   {
   }
   ```
3. Return a *404 Not Found* status code if no record matches the passed-in id. Use the **Exists** method you just added to check if the record exists.
   ```
   if (!_rep.Exists<Publisher>(id)) return NotFound();
   ```
4. Fetch the publisher to delete by calling the **Get** method with the **SqlDbContext** object.
   ```
   var entityToDelete = _rep.Get<Publisher>(id);
   ```
5. Call the **Delete** method you just added to remove the record from the database. Return a *500 Internal Server Error* status code if something goes wrong when persisting the changes.
   ```
   _rep.Delete(entityToDelete);

   if (!_rep.Save()) return StatusCode(500,
       "A problem occurred while handling your request.");
   ```
6. Return a *204 No Content* status code to show that the changes were persisted successfully.
   ```
   return NoContent();
   ```
7. Save all files.
8. Open the **Publishers** table in the database and decide which publisher to remove. Check that the publisher has books related to it in the **Books** table.

9. Select **DELETE** in Postman's drop-down.
10. Enter the URL to the **Delete** action.
    http://localhost:55098/api/genpublishers/1

11. Click the **Send** button in Postman. A *204 No Content* status code should be returned to Postman.
12. Close browser to stop the application.
13. Open the **Publishers** table again and refresh its data to make sure that the publisher was removed.
14. Open the **Books** table and make sure that the books related to the removed publisher were deleted.

The complete code for the **Delete** action in the **GenPublishersController** class:

```
[HttpDelete("{id}")]
public IActionResult Delete(int id)
{
    if (!_rep.Exists<Publisher>(id)) return NotFound();

    var entityToDelete = _rep.Get<Publisher>(id);

    _rep.Delete(entityToDelete);

    if (!_rep.Save()) return StatusCode(500,
        "A problem occurred while handling your request.");

    return NoContent();
}
```

Deleting a Book (DELETE)

When deleting a book related to a publisher, the publisher should not be removed from the **Publishers** table. Only the child-record, the book, should be deleted.

1. Open the **GenPublishersController** class.
2. Copy the **Delete** action you just added.
3. Open the **GenBooksController** class.
4. Paste in the **Delete** action you copied.
5. Change the URI in the **[HttpDelete]** attribute to: *{publisherId}/books/{id}*.
   ```
   [HttpDelete("{publisherId}/books/{id}")]
   ```
6. Add a **publisherId (int)** parameter at the beginning of the action method's parameter list.
   ```
   public IActionResult Delete(int publisherId, int id)
   ```

7. Change the defining type to **Book** for the **Exists** and **Get** methods.
```
if (!_rep.Exists<Book>(id)) return NotFound();
var entityToDelete = _rep.Get<Book>(id);
```

8. Save all files.

9. Open the **Books** table in the database and choose a book id for a book to delete. Note the publisher id; you will need it later.

10. Select **DELETE** in Postman's drop-down.

11. Enter the URL to the **Delete** action.

    http://localhost:55098/api/genpublishers/2/books/1

12. Click the **Send** button. A *204 No Content* status code should be returned to Postman.

13. Close the browser to stop the application.

14. Open the **Books** table again and refresh its data to make sure that the book was deleted. Open the **Publishers** table and refresh its content. The publisher that the book was related to should not have been removed.

The complete code for the **Delete** action in the **GenBooksController** class:

```
[HttpDelete("{publisherId}/books/{id}")]
public IActionResult Delete(int publisherId, int id)
{
    if (!_rep.Exists<Book>(id)) return NotFound();

    var entityToDelete = _rep.Get<Book>(id);

    _rep.Delete(entityToDelete);

    if (!_rep.Save()) return StatusCode(500,
        "A problem occurred while handling your request.");

    return NoContent();
}
```

Summary

In this chapter, you completed the implementation of the generic service that fetches data from an SQL Server database using Entity Framework Core. You also used Postman to request data from the Web API by calling the actions you added to the **GenBooksController** and **GenPublishersController** classes.

This is the last chapter in the book. I sincerely hope you enjoyed reading it and implementing the code.

Jonas Fagerberg

Other Titles by the Author

The author has written other books and produced video courses that you might find helpful.

Books by the Author

Below is a list if the most recent books by the author. The books are available on Amazon.

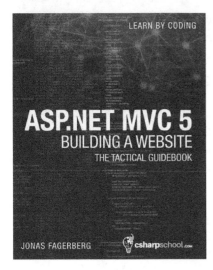

ASP.NET Core 1.1 – Building a Website: http://www.amazon.com/dp/1546832068

ASP.NET MVC 5 – Building a Website: www.amazon.com/dp/B01IF63FIY

C# for Beginners: https://www.amazon.com/dp/B017OAFR8I

Store Secret Data in .NET Core Web App with Azure Key Vault (video course)
In this Udemy course you will learn how to store sensitive data in a secure manner. First you will learn how to store data securely in a file called *secrets.json* with the User Manager. The file is stored locally on your machine, outside the project's folder structure. It is therefore not checked into your code repository. Then you will learn how to use Azure Web App Settings to store key-value pairs for a specific web application. The third and final way to secure your sensitive data is using Azure Key Vault, secured with Azure Active Directory in the cloud.

The course is taught using an ASP.NET Core 1.1 Web API solution in Visual Studio 2015 and Visual Studio 2017.

You really need to know this if you are a serious developer.

You can watch this video course on Udemy at this URL:
www.udemy.com/store-secret-data-in-net-core-web-app-with-azure-key-vault

MVC 5 – How to Build a Membership Website (video course)
This is a comprehensive video course on how to build a membership site using ASP.NET MVC 5. The course has more than **24 hours** of video.

In this video course, you will learn how to build a membership website from scratch. You will create the database using Entity Framework code-first, scaffold an Administrator UI, and build a front-end UI using HTML5, CSS3, Bootstrap, JavaScript, C#, and MVC 5. Prerequisites for this course are: a good knowledge of the C# language and basic knowledge of MVC 5, HTML5, CSS3, Bootstrap, and JavaScript.

You can watch this video course on Udemy at this URL:
www.udemy.com/building-a-mvc-5-membership-website